Homefront
Arkansas
Arkansans Face Wartime

ON THE COVER: Workers at the Jacksonville Ordnance Plant pose with an American flag. During World War II, the plant produced 88 percent of the detonators and fuses used by Allied forces in the war effort. At one point, more than 14,000 workers—most of them women—were employed at the plant in central Arkansas. Photo courtesy of the Butler Center for Arkansas Studies.

VELMA B. BRANSCUM WOODY AND STEVEN TESKE

Homefront Arkansas
Arkansans Face Wartime

BUTLER CENTER BOOKS

Butler Center Books
Little Rock, Arkansas

BUTLER
CENTER **butlercenterbooks.org**

The Butler Center for Arkansas Studies
Central Arkansas Library System
100 Rock Street
Little Rock, Arkansas 72201

BOOKS

First edition, November 2009

ISBN 978-0-9800897-9-0 (10-digit 0-9800897-9-0)

10 9 8 7 6 5 4 3 2 1

PROJECT MANAGER: Rod Lorenzen
BOOK COVER DESIGN: Wendell E. Hall
PAGE DESIGN AND COMPOSITION: Shelly Culbertson
COPYEDITOR: Ali Welky
PROOFREADER: Annie Stricklin

Library of Congress Cataloging-in-Publication Data

Woody, Velma B. Branscum.
  Homefront Arkansas: Arkansans face wartime / by Velma B. Branscum Woody and Steven Teske. -- 1st ed.
    p. cm.
  ISBN 978-0-9800897-9-0 (pbk. : alk. paper)
  1. Arkansas--History, Military--Juvenile literature. 2. War and society--Arkansas--History--Juvenile literature. 3. Children and war--Arkansas--History--Juvenile literature. 4. Arkansas--Social conditions--Juvenile literature. I. Teske, Steven. II. Title.

  F411.3.W66 2009
  355.009767--dc22
                          2009045823

Printed in the United States of America

This book is printed on archival-quality paper that meets requirements of The American National Standard for Information Sciences, Permanence of Paper, Printed Library Materials, ANSI Z39.48-1984.

ACKNOWLEDGEMENTS

I wish to thank my family, especially my son-in-law Sean Steiger and daughter-in-law Keli Woody, who worked so diligently to help me create this book, as well as Ted Parkhurst and Rod Lorenzen at Butler Center Books, who were so patient and helpful throughout this process. I especially want to thank my parents, Thurlow and Mamie Branscum, as well as Charlie Branscum, my grandfather, who gave me the love of history, especially Arkansas history. —VW

I would like to thank my fellow workers at the Butler Center for Arkansas Studies, especially those on the staff of the Encyclopedia of Arkansas History & Culture (Nathania Sawyer, Guy Lancaster, Anna Lancaster, Mike Polston, Ali Welky, and Mike Keckhaver). Their encouragement and suggestions were extremely valuable. I also would like to thank my wife Robin, as well as my children, who read these chapters at various stages and gave many helpful comments. —ST

TABLE OF CONTENTS

chapter 1

LETTERS FROM THE BATTLEFIELD: THE MEXICAN WAR

Thirteen-year-old Rebecca Brown gazed out the front window of her great-grandmother's home, wondering how to spend her afternoon. Her family had come by, as they did every autumn, to help with the hog slaughter. The process of killing the hog and preparing the meat made Rebecca a little more squeamish each year. This year, even before the killing began, Rebecca excused herself and escaped into her great-grandmother's house.

Granny (as everyone called Rebecca's great-grandmother) and Granny's parents had lived near Batesville when they first came to Arkansas, just two years before it changed from a territory to a state. They had farmed the rich soil near the White River, prospering most years, but suffering occasionally from devastating floods. Later they had moved to Oil Trough, where Rebecca found herself this year of 1920.

Rebecca was not, by nature, a girl who looked for trouble, but left alone in the house, given no instructions from her elders, Rebecca could think of nothing useful to do. Granny had always told her to keep busy at doing useful things. "Idle hands are the devil's playground," Granny often said. Now Rebecca asked herself, how did Granny keep her hands busy during those rare times when she had nothing to cook or clean or sew? Rebecca had often seen Granny sitting at the kitchen table, playing a card game she called Patience. Granny had even taken the time, on a rainy day last spring, to explain to Rebecca the rules of the one-person game. Rebecca was sure that she could remember the rules of the game, if only she could get her hands on that deck of cards. Looking at the bureau in the corner of the living room, Rebecca wondered if Granny's card deck might be kept inside. Even before she had time to ask herself whether Granny would mind what she was doing, Rebecca pulled open the top drawer of the bureau and peered inside, hoping to see the tattered paper box in which the cards were kept.

Instead of seeing the box of cards, Rebecca found a store of other treasures: buttons and spools of thread and needles Granny used in her sewing, Granny's spare pair of eyeglasses, several odds and ends that Rebecca could not quickly identify, and the stationery and steel-tipped pens Granny used when she wrote letters to her family. Gingerly, Rebecca pushed these items aside, hoping that the cards would appear underneath them. Instead, her hands brushed against a stack of fragile yellow papers tied together with a faded yellow ribbon. Clearly, Granny had been saving letters from a long time ago, letters written when she was much younger. Again, Rebecca did not stop to ask herself if Granny would approve. Gently, careful not to tear the old paper or let it crumble in her hands, Rebecca slid the top letter out of the package and took it near the window where she could read it.

"October 1, 1846," was written neatly at the top of the page, and underneath read, "Dearest Sis." Quickly she glanced out the window to make sure no one was coming toward the house, and then she continued reading.

Still we sit in San Antonio, deep in the heart of Texas, finding ourselves bored with nothing to do. We wait for our orders to move out, but we have been here already more than a month. Colonel Archibald Yell, our former governor and former congressman, was elected to lead us when we gathered up in Washington, Arkansas, during the summer, but some of the men are starting to grumble and say that he does not lead. We had been told, before we voted, that Mister Yell was a war hero, having served with Andrew Jackson in 1814 and later in the Indian wars. Yet in all these weeks he has done nothing to whip the troops into shape. For the most part, the soldiers are undisciplined. They drink and they fight one another. It is nothing for a fight to break out with six or seven men participating. They will be playing cards for pennies, and one or more will shout out in anger, and then the blood will fly. I have got so that I will not even play checkers with any man. Our living conditions are terrible. When it is dry, the dust blows, and when it rains, mud and muck are everywhere. Most of us sleep by our horses on the horse blankets, which are cleaner than anything else we have. A few men have tried to wash themselves in the river, but most do not bother. General Wool, I am told, has taken to calling us Yell's Mounted Devils.

You wouldn't find Texas at all pretty. The trees are snaggly and ugly. Because the horses trample the river banks, the water is muddy and murky. It seems that one day just runs into the next. All the soldiers from Arkansas are so unorganized that nothing gets done properly. My horse, Ranger, stands here now and nuzzles my neck. He is anxious to begin riding, because he too is bored. We have enough to eat, mostly beans and fatback. We expect that we will fight soon. Our troops are rough and are in no way disciplined soldiers. We could pass the time better if someone would whip the troops into shape. I miss you very much, Sis, and I miss John and Jacob and Andy, and of course Mother and Father. I thought traveling would be exciting, but now I just wish I was home.

Your loving brother,
Robert

Rebecca had just read the signature on the letter when she heard footsteps on the wooden porch behind the back door. She dropped the letter into the bureau drawer and slipped it closed, then whirled to see her mother crossing the kitchen, heading into the front room. "Are you all right, darling?" her mother asked.

"Yes, Mother, I'm fine," Rebecca assured her, as her fingers twitched to get to the rest of the letters in the short stack. She knew that her mother would not stay in the house long, not with so much work to be done outdoors.

Ever since the family had come to Arkansas, nearly a century ago, they had raised and killed two or three hogs each year to provide meat and other supplies for the coming year. Granny liked to boast that they "used every part of the pig except the squeal." Meat was salted and put aside for the winter, except for the choicest cut, which would be cooked and eaten that weekend as part of the annual festivities. The feet of the pig would be boiled for soup stock, while fat was boiled to use for soap or set aside to use in cooking for the next few weeks. The skin and even various inner parts of the animal all had their purpose, and most of the family was involved, one way or another, in turning the hog into useable portions.

"I feel odd leaving you indoors with nothing to do," her mother remarked. "Don't you at least want to sit on the porch where you can see and hear the rest of the family?"

"Don't worry about me, please," Rebecca answered. "I was just sitting in here, imagining how things used to be years ago. I promise that if I get lonely, I'll come back outside."

Mother calmly looked at Rebecca for a short time, then smiled and said, "That's fine, darling. I trust you. Enjoy your trip into the past." With a graceful wave of her hand, Mother turned and left by way of the kitchen and the porch. In an instant, Rebecca had the bureau drawer open and the letters back in her hand. She slipped the other sheets out from the yellow ribbon. Finding the second letter, she carried it delicately to the window and began to read.

October 9, 1846

Dearest Sis,

Yesterday we finally received our orders and began to travel into Mexico. We have crossed a river called the Rio Grande and are in a region that is spelled Chihuahua but pronounced 'Cheewa-wa.' The troops still are very undisciplined. They yell and fight and threaten one another most of the time. One of our Arkansas soldiers even threatened General Wool. He burst into the general's tent, waving a gun. I am amazed that he was not arrested and hanged. General Wool and Colonel Yell argue a great deal. Captain Pike seems to get along better with the general. Both of them see that the troops need more discipline. After just two days of travel, my horse is already tired, and I am suffering from sores being back in the saddle after so many weeks away from it. When I dismount I am so stiff that I can hardly walk when I hit the ground. I am exhausted. The pace is too hard. Food is becoming scarce, and I am beginning to feel hunger. We ran out of beans three days ago. We are lucky now to be given cornmeal gruel twice a day. I thought we could at least hunt a little, but shooting of any kind is strictly forbidden. They never know where the Mexican soldiers might be located. One gunshot could lead to an ambush on our troops. I would give a hundred dollars this evening for a plate of fresh-killed pork and some freshly baked cornbread.

Your loving brother,
Robert

"Is all well with you, child?" The gentle voice of her great-grandmother startled Rebecca from her reading. Shame glowed in her cheeks as Rebecca realized that she had no way to hide what she was doing. The bureau drawer was open, and the precious letters were spread before her on the floor.

"Granny, I'm so sorry," Rebecca moaned as tears slipped from the corners of her eyes. "I didn't mean to pry. I was only looking for your cards so I could play Patience, but I found these letters instead. I never even knew that you had a brother named Robert."

Granny sighed as she settled into her favorite rocker in the front room. "Child, you were wrong to open my drawers and touch my things, and I wish you had not touched these letters. I've been afraid for years to handle them, fearing that they might fall to pieces. I see that you have been careful with them, though. I forgive you, child."

"Oh, thank you, Granny," Rebecca exclaimed. "But tell me, please, more about your brother."

Granny began to rock thoughtfully as she answered Rebecca's question. "Robert never wanted to stay on the farm with the rest of the family. He told us that his dream was to travel and see more of the world, rather than taming the frontier. When the war with Mexico began and the president was calling for volunteers to fight, Robert begged permission to take his horse and join the other soldiers. Father didn't want to say yes, but I gather he knew that Robert would never be a farmer. Robert rode to Washington and became part of the Regiment of Mounted Gunmen from Arkansas. Of course, he had learned at home how to ride a horse and shoot a gun. Father had also taught him the importance of working together with the family and of following orders. I knew from his letters that he was sorely disappointed with many of his fellow soldiers."

Rebecca found the third letter on the floor beside her. "Do you want me to read aloud, Granny?" she asked.

"Yes, child," Granny replied. "Let me hear again my brother's voice, even in your girlish speaking."

Rebecca began to read the letter.

December 15, 1846

Dearest Sis,

I am past the point of exhaustion. My feet are sore and bleeding as my shoes are almost in tatters. I had to wrap rawhide strips around them or I could never hold them on my feet. I am now a member of General Wool's army under the command of Captain Pike. Two weeks ago, General Wool arrested all our officers, one by one, after Colonel Yell refused to camp at the place that the general had chosen. It took time to sort that out, and all the soldiers wondered what we would do without our chosen officers. We have made a brutal march, covering more than 100 miles in just three days. We still are in Chihuahua, but we are continuing to march. Only the Good Lord knows where we will end up. They tell us that the Mexican army, led by Santa Anna, is on the way to Buena Vista. We are to reinforce the main American army which is already there. So I know we will go there first. I am so starved and weary, Sis. I am now a foot soldier. My horse was shot two weeks ago. A Mexican rifleman shot him from under me while I was on guard patrol. I did everything I could to save Ranger, but he was hurt too badly. I didn't know I could miss an animal so much. I do not know if I can fight if we see Santa Anna and his army. May God give me strength. Give my greetings to Ted, my childhood companion. Perhaps you and he will have news for the family by the time I return home.

Your loving brother,
Robert

Granny continued rocking slowly, a thoughtful expression on her face. "Granny," Rebecca asked as she set the letter aside, "who was Ted?"

"Why, honey!" Granny said with a sudden smile. "Ted was your great-grandfather. His name was Theodore, but we called him Ted or Teddy back then."

"Oh," said Rebecca. "So Great-Great-Uncle Robert knew him too?"

"Yes, honey." Again Granny smiled. "He was Robert's best friend. Robert was the one who introduced me to him. If it hadn't been for me, Teddy would have gone with Robert, and you and your father and grandmother might never have been born."

"Really?" exclaimed Rebecca. "I had no idea. I'm learning a lot today."

Granny nodded and rocked gently as memories of Ted filled her mind.

Rebecca took another letter and began to read.

January 25, 1847

Dearest Sis,

I was right. We are now at Buena Vista. The weather is brutal here, and the soldiers feel threatened from every side. We know that we are outnumbered, and still we lack supplies and discipline. My shoes have even bigger holes in them, and my clothing is almost to the point of rags. I found that I can live on very little to eat and can keep on going on little rest. A few of the men have been able to forage some vegetables from the countryside. This diet is hurting my stomach. I have never wanted to be home as badly as I want it now. If I ever get back, I know I will not leave again. I will be so glad to eat your home cooking once more.

Today I stood guard without my horse for twelve hours. This was grueling. General Wool is expecting the Mexican army any day. The night before last, Major Borland was captured with nearly three dozen soldiers because they hadn't bothered to post a guard. I expect I will be on patrol again tomorrow. It will be another day of the same. War is not exciting, Sis. All I see is hunger, pain, and fear. Fighting among the troops continues every night. I get so tired of it. I have two or three friends that stay around. We just stay away from the other troops. My friends, though, live in fear of being captured by the Mexican soldiers. They tell fearful stories of torture. I tell them not to worry. I am sure that the Mexican soldiers will be no more cruel to us than we would be to them. Please pray for me and for all our soldiers here.

Your loving brother,
Robert

Neither Granny nor Rebecca said anything until Rebecca found the last letter and began to read.

February 25, 1847

Dearest Sis,

I have finally seen war in Mexico, and I pray that I never see it again. Four days ago, we were ordered to remove supplies from Agua Nueva ahead of Santa Anna's approaching army. We burned whatever we could not carry so the Mexicans could not have those things. That was horrible. You know we didn't want to part with the few supplies we had left. We are now facing complete starvation even if we survive. Santa Anna arrived at Buena Vista with a huge army. Our numbers have dwindled because of sickness and poor food. We started with more than 800 men, but at the start of the battle we had only 479. Now brace yourself for some distressing news. Colonel Yell was killed in the battle. He had charged into a group of Mexican lancers and was cut to pieces. Some men said that he was rallying the troops with great courage, but others say that he lost control of his horse. I was one of the 250 dismounted Arkansans on the mountain to the left of Yell's troops. We were not able to help them in time. The fighting ebbed and flowed all morning. The lancers continued to advance, even after Colonel Yell fell. Some of our soldiers ran from the attack. God help us all. I received a wound from a bullet in my left leg, but, Sis, do not worry about me. I know I will recover, and perhaps this wound will spare me from having to continue in this war. Please remember that I love you all, and my fondest wish is to be back home, working on the farm again.

Your loving brother,
Robert

Rebecca looked up at Granny and saw tears in her eyes. "Granny," she said as gently as she could, "was Robert right? Did he return from the war?"

"No, child." Granny hesitated, as if she was struggling to control her voice. Finally, she said, "The Arkansas regiment, then under Colonel Roane, returned home in June of 1847. Very few bodies came back with them, and Robert's was not one of them. His leg wound rapidly grew worse in Mexico, and they waited too long to cut off the leg. Two days later he was dead, and they buried him there, near the battlefield. He had wanted to come home so badly. I was sorry that he could not be buried here with his family."

Rebecca stood and wrapped her arms around Granny. "I'm so sorry, Granny. I didn't mean to bring back such painful memories. I was wrong."

In spite of her tears, Granny managed a small chuckle. "I've already forgiven you once, child. I do not need to say it again. It is an honor to Robert that you wanted to know about him. He would be very proud to be remembered. Robert was vibrant and full of life. All he ever wanted to do was to see the world. He was excited at the thought of travel, but he was unlucky in that war. Still, he made his family proud. Our parents were grief-stricken when they learned of his loss, but they still were proud of him as well."

Granny hugged Rebecca. "Now, Rebecca, you can be proud of your great-great-uncle also. Because you have read his letters, I feel like you knew him too. This will please me greatly. I can talk to you now about my brother, and you will understand what I am saying. This will help me too. Yes, it was wrong of you to read my letters, but good has come out of your mischief."

The War with Mexico—sometimes called the Mexican-American War or the Mexican War—followed from the secession of Texas from Mexico in 1836 and the annexation of Texas by the United States in 1845. Battles between U.S. forces and Mexican forces near the Rio Grande led the United States to declare war on Mexico on May 13, 1846. The war effectively ended when U.S. troops occupied Mexico City on September 14, 1847. About 116,000 soldiers from the United States—including more than 73,000 volunteers—served in the war, although many soldiers saw no action. Mexico had fewer than 40,000 soldiers in its army at the time. The United States suffered 1,177 deaths and 3,669 injured, while Mexico had 12,866 killed and many more injured. On both sides, more men died from disease than from battle injuries. Roughly 1,500 soldiers from Arkansas fought in the war; precise numbers of those who died or were wounded are not available.

chapter 2

THE DAY THE THUNDER DIED AT POISON SPRINGS: THE CIVIL WAR

Jesse Hawk sat on the front porch, listening to the huge cannons still firing in the dusky dark. Sometimes, sparks would fly through the air as the cannonballs left the barrels.

The night was April 17, 1864. Jesse had just turned thirteen years old. He and his mother lived with his grandmother about fourteen miles from Camden, Arkansas. The area was called Poison Springs, but Jesse did not know why it had that name. So far as he knew, none of the natural springs in the area was poisonous. Jesse and his mother had moved from Indian Territory after his father had joined Stand Watie's First Cherokee Mounted Volunteers. At first, the family had thought that the two of them would be safer in southern Arkansas than in the west. Without his father there, though, they found that they could barely keep the little family alive on the farm. Workers were few, because most able-bodied men had gone off to fight in the Civil War.

Like the other farmers of the area, Jesse and his mother and grandmother had managed to harvest some corn the previous fall, but, in the last two days, Northern soldiers had invaded the farms and carried off all the stored corn they could find. They had also seized two legs of venison that the three of them had been eating on sparingly to stave off hunger, hoping the meat would last and not spoil. They had already lost all their farm animals except for Bessie, their milk cow. She had escaped the attention of soldiers and bandits because she frequently wandered away from the farm and hid in the swampy woods nearby. Jesse hoped she was safely hidden there now. He wondered how he and his mother and grandmother would survive with the corn and venison stolen and with little hope of getting a crop planted that spring.

Jesse was startled out of his reverie by his mother's voice.

"Jesse," she whispered, "why don't you come to bed? The battle might last all night!"

"Ma!" Jesse turned a worried face to his mother. "I know the Yankees are close to this house. But what if one of the Rebels is Dad?"

"I know, son," sighed his mother. "I'm scared too. But, son, your dad is in Georgia. That's a long way from here."

Jesse silently nodded, somewhat soothed. He quietly went up to his bed, but he could hardly sleep. The huge guns continued to shake the house as they boomed like thunder in the night. The Rebel soldiers had set up an ambush on the highway that ran between Camden and Washington. They had managed to trap some of the same Union soldiers who had been stealing corn and other food from the farms. Screams and yells sifted through the trees as the seemingly endless night dragged on, hour after slow hour.

Jesse arose at the break of dawn, surprised that he had even managed to fall asleep. Strangely, the big guns were silent. No creature or bird could be heard. The air was still. The stench of smoke and fire lingered in the air along with the sweet, coppery smell of blood.

Jesse decided to go get old Bessie. He thought he could hear her bell faintly ringing in the woods up to the left of the house. Jesse hoped to bring her safely home before any of the wandering soldiers from either army found her. He decided to let the two women sleep while he went after the cow.

Jesse walked along, trying to be as quiet as possible. It seemed the longer he walked, the farther away the cowbell sounded. The rank smell of blood and smoke became stronger and stronger. Suddenly, Jesse stopped dead still. What he had stumbled upon took his breath away.

A terrible scene was before him. He had to bend to the ground, holding his mouth, to stop the scream bubbling up in his throat. About a hundred black Federal troops lay on the ground, sprinkled with a few white soldiers, both Yankees and Rebels. They were all dead or dying. Many had arms or legs missing. The way some crawled on the ground in the terrible throes of death made them look like wounded animals of a horrifying species unimaginable to mankind. The uniforms on the men were ragged and torn, red with blood.

Jesse jumped as he heard the sharp report of a rifle. He looked up in astonishment at a group of Confederate soldiers firing, seemingly without feeling, at the dying men, shooting them one by one. They were killing the injured black soldiers, even the ones strong enough to surrender.

He began to back up deeper and deeper into the woods. He did not want the Rebels to spot him. He forgot old Bessie as he moved silently backward until he could no longer see the dead and dying soldiers, and then he sank to the ground. His whole body trembled, and he felt like he was going to be sick. He took several breaths and finally began to feel a little better.

Suddenly, he heard voices. He was stunned—there were two Confederate soldiers standing at the edge of the battlefield.

"Oh God, help me!" Jesse prayed. "I didn't get as far away as I thought I did. They will catch me now for sure!"

He sat perfectly still. He looked around frantically and realized that he had made a half circle in the woods. He had been so terrified that he had lost his sense of direction and was on another side of the battlefield. The men he had heard talking were Rebel officers.

The first officer said in a deadly calm voice, "The ambush succeeded, but it was closer than it should have been. We were lucky to have more men, as well as the element of surprise. If we hadn't had these cannons and the Indian brigades, those Yankees would have whipped us good."

"Yeah," the other officer grunted. "Those blacks sure know how to fight. But we've made sure this group won't fight us again, I bet you."

The officers slapped each other on the shoulder and walked away, seeming proud as could be of what they had done.

Jesse stood stunned. He couldn't understand why the Rebels shot the men instead of taking them as prisoners of war. They had even shot those who were trying to surrender.

Jesse immediately tried to backtrack to the path he took earlier in the morning. He slowly moved back through the woods until he was sure he knew where he was. He began to hear old Bessie again and made his way down to the cow.

Old Bessie was standing near the creek, munching the green grass growing on the creek bank. As Jesse neared the creek, he saw a black soldier lying on his stomach reaching up with his hand and milking the cow. He was spraying the milk into his mouth. The man was severely wounded. His left hand was swollen purple and appeared broken. His back and legs were covered with blood. His uniform was in ribbons from crawling and walking through the briars and woods. Jesse walked up to the cow and startled the man.

He said, "Sir, are you hurt badly?"

The man turned his head, gasping. "Yes," he said, "my left hand is broken. I've lost so much blood, I can hardly stand. My left leg is cut badly, I think."

Jesse said, "Can you walk if I help you?"

"Maybe," said the soldier.

"If you can, I'll take you to my house. My Ma will set your hand and try to bandage your leg to stop the bleeding."

"What makes you think that your ma would help an enemy soldier, especially a black one?" the soldier sneered angrily.

"Because my Ma will help anybody. She wouldn't want me to let you stay here and die in the woods."

"Well, okay," the soldier sighed. "I've got nothing to lose."

Jesse helped the man to his feet and then slowly made his way back to the farm. The soldier leaned heavily on Jesse, so heavily that at times Jesse seemed almost to be carrying him. Jesse's mother came running as soon as she saw Jesse and the soldier. She had been worried terribly when she awoke and found Jesse gone. She had imagined him taken prisoner, or possibly even killed in the fighting.

"Jesse, what happened? What are you doing? Who is this?" his mother half yelled, breathless.

Jesse told his mother about stumbling onto the battlefield looking for old Bessie. She looked astonished as she listened to his story.

He said, "Ma, can you help him?"

"I'll try, Jesse—all I can do is try, but we will have to hide him down at the springhouse until this dies down. But we must feed him first—give him enough strength to make it down there."

Grandma prepared their usual cornmeal gruel for breakfast, spoon-feeding the soldier, though he ate little. Afterward, the three of them carefully led the soldier deep into the woods to the springhouse. The soldier was so weak he could hardly walk, even with the support of all three of them. When they got him to the bed, he fainted.

"Well," said Ma, "maybe that is for the best. He needs to sleep while I set the broken hand."

She cleaned and set the broken hand. Grandma and Jesse removed the blood-soaked, torn uniform and carefully cleaned his other wounds. There was one deep cut on his left leg, but Ma thought it would heal. Still, the soldier remained unconscious. She bound the wound after plastering it with a poultice. They had done everything they could.

The next three days, the soldier suffered. He tossed and turned with a high fever. Grandma continued to feed him, while Ma changed the bandages twice a day.

Finally, on the fourth day, the soldier opened his eyes. He was very weak, but he could feed himself and sit up in bed for a little while. He told them his name was Buddy—Buddy Duke. He said he had a wife and three children in the state of Kansas.

"I can only hope to go back to them soon," Buddy sighed. He owned a small farm there.

Jesse introduced himself. "My name is Jesse Hawk. This is my mother, Mary Hawk, and my grandmother, Emma Hawk. My dad is John Hawk. We are a very few of the Cherokee Indians who are left in Arkansas."

The soldier looked sad for a moment. "I was twelve years old when my parents left the South. My dad's old master set us free just before he died. The law said that if we stayed, we would be sold again as slaves. That's why we moved to Kansas."

Each day, the soldier became stronger. He began to eat more and could walk for longer and longer periods of time. His hand was healing nicely. Two weeks later, Buddy was ready to return to his regiment.

Standing in front of the house, he told Jesse, "I will tell my sons and my grandsons of your great generosity. You people saved my life and for that I will be eternally grateful." And then he strode through the woods, looking for the nearby Northern army.

The Civil War began April 12, 1861, with shots fired at Fort Sumter, South Carolina. Arkansas seceded from the United States less than a month later, on May 6, 1861. The war ended on April 9, 1865, with the surrender of General Robert E. Lee at Appomattox, Virginia, but many Arkansas soldiers did not surrender until the next month, the last of them surrendering on June 2, 1865. In all, the four-year war resulted in the deaths of 389,753 Union soldiers and 289,000 Confederate soldiers. A further 275,175 Union soldiers and 194,026 Confederate soldiers were wounded on the battlefields. Roughly 180,000 African-American soldiers, including 94,000 former slaves, served in the Union army during the Civil War. About one third of them died during the conflict.

Major Civil War battles fought in Arkansas include those at Pea Ridge, Prairie Grove, Arkansas Post, and Helena; in all, more than 700 engagements between Union and Confederate forces happened in the state. As many as 60,000 Confederate soldiers and 15,000 Union soldiers came from Arkansas. Roughly 10,000 of these soldiers died in the war, and thousands more were injured. Roughly 1,500 African-American soldiers from Arkansas died as a result of injuries during the war.

chapter 3

A HOUSE DIVIDED: THE BROOKS-BAXTER WAR

The men stood around Bill Maxwell's grocery store in Little Rock, the way they did every weekday around noon, and swapped stories as they chewed their tobacco. Fourteen-year-old Joe Maxwell swept the floor, eager to stay close and listen to the men. Sometimes they talked about weather and storms they could remember—floods and ice storms and tornadoes. Sometimes they talked about hunting trips they had shared, and boasted of the deer and bears and other large animals they had killed, or regaled each other with tall tales about fish they had caught. At least a couple times a week, though, the men's memories went back to the great War Between the States and the way they had fought to defend Arkansas from the Yankees. Hearing their tales, Joe could scarcely believe that Arkansas had been on the losing side of the war. He knew from school, of course, that Arkansas had tried to leave the Union and that the Civil War had preserved the Union, so that Arkansas was still today one of the United States. As his ears soaked in the heroic tales told by these veteran soldiers, though, Joe could almost convince himself that they had won the war and kept Arkansas free from Northern interference.

Today was no different from other days, and after working all summer in the grocery store, Joe could repeat the stories he had heard almost word for word. The year was 1894, and already some veterans of the war were dying of illnesses or just old age. As the store's visitors left one by one, Joe decided it was time to ask his father a question that had been teasing in the back of his mind for several weeks. "Dad," he said as he set the broom back in the corner and climbed onto a stool, "why don't you ever tell war stories with the men who come into the store? You tell fishing

Bill Maxwell bought meat to barbecue from Kindervater's Butcher Shop on Ninth Street in Little Rock, shown here in 1897. Photo courtesy of Virginia Kindervater.

stories and hunting stories with the rest of them; why don't you ever talk about the war?"

Dad laughed as he answered. "Son, I don't tell stories about the war because I was just a baby when that war started. All those men who come into the store at noon are older than me, and all of them fought in the war and survived. Your uncle Dave and I would be fibbing if we told stories like theirs, because we never fought."

"So you aren't a war hero like your customers?"

Bill Maxwell must have heard the disappointment in his son's voice. Reaching across the counter, he rumpled Joe's hair and said, "The truth is, I do have a small war story to share. It doesn't go back to the War Between the States, but when I was a boy—exactly the age you are now—I wore a uniform and marched on the streets of Little Rock with Governor Elisha Baxter."

"Wow! Was there a war in Little Rock that made you march with Governor Baxter?"

"There was a war here in Arkansas, a little war that didn't spread to other states. Maybe that's why you haven't heard people talking about it before now. The Brooks-Baxter War was pretty amazing when it happened, though, and I'm one of those who can say that I played a part in the war."

"How did it start, Dad?"

"Well, back in 1872, there were two men who were running for governor of Arkansas. One was Mr. Joseph Brooks, and the other was Mr. Elisha Baxter."

Joe knew a few things about elections, because the men in the store were always talking about the last election or the next election. "Which of them was the Democrat, and which was the Republican?" he asked, trying to show his father that he understood what he had heard about politics. Joe had heard men in the store talk about other groups, like the Populists, but he knew that most elections had a Democrat and a Republican.

"Actually, Joe, both men were Republicans."

"Both of them?" This was a new matter for Joe's mind. As far back as he could remember, the Democrats had nominated a man for governor, and, after the general election, he had been the governor. One time, the Republicans hadn't even bothered to nominate a man for governor. "Are you sure they were both Republicans, Dad? I've never heard of such a thing."

Bill Maxwell laughed. "I've never heard of such a thing" was a usual response in the shop when his customers exchanged tall tales about hunting or fishing or weather.

He said, "Yes, Joe, both of them were Republicans. Things were different in Arkansas after the war. Many Democrats were not allowed to vote or to run for office for a while, because they had fought against the Union. A lot of people came in from the North to help run things for a while. Your grandparents and a lot of other people called them 'carpetbaggers' and called the Southerners who cooperated with them 'scalawags.' The Republicans won a lot of elections during those years, but, by 1872, there were two groups of Republicans who didn't agree with each other about a lot of things. Both groups nominated a man to be governor, and so Mr. Baxter and Mr. Brooks wound up running against each other.

When all the ballots were counted, the counters said that Mr. Baxter had gotten more votes than Mr. Brooks. Mr. Brooks and his supporters said that they believed a mistake had been made in the counting. They were sure that Mr. Brooks had won the

election. In fact, they were accusing Mr. Baxter and his side of
cheating, since his group of Republicans had been in charge of
counting the ballots. Mr. Baxter moved into the State House and
began his job as governor, but meanwhile Mr. Brooks spent the
next few weeks and months in courtrooms, trying to find a judge
who would throw out the election results and say that Mr. Brooks
would be governor."

"Did Mr. Brooks find a judge who agreed with him?" Joe
asked, but instead of answering the question, his father held up
a hand.

"Did you hear something out back?" he whispered.

Joe shook his head.

"Let's check," Dad said. Grabbing a wooden club he kept
under the counter in the store, he led Joe past the shelves of
supplies and out to the small yard behind the store where he
cooked his barbecued beef and pork to sell.

From the doorway, they looked out into the yard, but no one
was there. Joe breathed a sigh of relief, then quickly breathed
deeply through his nose. He loved the smell of his father's barbecued meats, and he knew that the meat was one of the main
items that brought people into his father's store six days a week.
Most people cooked meals for themselves and their families at
home, but some of the older men of Little Rock were glad to eat
the barbecue instead of having to cook for themselves too often.

Dad also breathed a sigh of relief.

"I'm always sure someone is trying to steal my barbecue,"
he said. "Lots of men in this town would love to steal my secret
recipe and make a lot of money selling what I sell. Why, even my
own brother would steal the recipe from me and go into business
for himself if he could."

"Is there a secret recipe to your barbecue, Dad?" Joe asked,
but his father pretended not to have heard him. They returned to
the store front, and Dad picked up the story of Brooks and Baxter
where he had left off.

"You asked if Mr. Brooks found a judge who would agree with
him. Well, it took until the middle of April 1874, but at last a
judge signed a paper saying that Mr. Brooks should be governor.
Before anyone else knew what was going on, Mr. Brooks and a

group of his supporters marched into the State House and drove Mr. Baxter out of his office. He hadn't been prepared for such an invasion, and he had no choice but to walk out of the building and look for a place where he could find some friends.

"He ended up at St. Johns' College down on Ninth Street. The school had been started before the war, then had been closed during the war, and now was open again. Your grandparents had sent me there, hoping to see me get an education, but St. Johns' was more of a military academy than any sort of college. It was right next to the Arsenal, which might be one reason he came to the school. Some of his supporters met him at the college, and they got weapons from the Arsenal. Right about sunset, his friends threw together a big parade, with him riding in a coach and all of us students marching in front of and behind his coach, wearing our school uniforms. Every block of the way, we picked up more Little Rock citizens who were on Mr. Baxter's side. He made his headquarters at the Anthony House, just down Markham Street from the State House, and declared martial law. That is how, by April 16, 1874, the state of Arkansas had two governors, and now you are free to say again that you never heard of such a thing."

"Well, I never have," Joe confessed. "So there were two men who said they were governor, and you wore a uniform and marched in a parade, but it really wasn't much of a war, was it? I mean, no shots were fired and no one got killed, so how could it have been a war?"

Dad said, "Well, wait, I haven't finished yet. As the news got out about what had happened, each man gathered more and more friends on his side, until there were at least a thousand men supporting Mr. Baxter and at least a thousand men supporting Mr. Brooks. The men supporting Mr. Brooks got two cannons and put them on the lawn of the State House, pointing at the Anthony House where Mr. Baxter was staying. Almost every man in Little Rock was carrying a gun, and the federal soldiers from the Arsenal were getting scared that they were going to see a shooting war break out in Little Rock.

"The first shots were fired on April 21. Mr. Baxter had given a speech, and lots of his supporters were shouting, and Mr. Brooks's supporters were shouting just as loud. I was in the crowd that day to hear the speech and cheer for Mr. Baxter, and I heard gunfire, but I never did find out which side fired first. All I know is that both sides were shooting at each other for a while, until the federal soldiers ran in to separate the crowd. Several people were hurt, some by bullets and some by broken glass and some just from the pushing of the crowd. That night, the soldiers started putting up barricades on the streets of Little Rock to keep the two sides apart, and we knew that a war had begun."

When his father paused, Joe heard the same noise his father had heard earlier, a rustling from behind the store. Both of them again rushed to the back of the store, only to see an unknown person leap the fence out of the back yard just before Joe and his father could get to the doorway. Bill Maxwell leaned in the doorway to catch his breath and shook a fist at the escaping spy.

When they returned once more to the store front, Joe asked his question again. "Do you really have a secret barbecue recipe?" he asked.

Dad looked at his son thoughtfully for a short time and then said, "Well, Joe, someday you'll be taking over the store and the business. I guess it's not too soon to share with you some of the secrets of the trade.

"Yes, I have a secret to making the perfect barbecue. In fact, I have three secrets, and anyone who wanted to copy my success would have to know all three. The first secret is to buy the best meat you can and never settle for second best. I always get my beef and pork from that German butcher shop near where I went to school, on Ninth Street. They have the best meat at the best price of any shop in town. Second, your mother and I have worked out a special blend of spices to cook with the meat. We don't just splash in vinegar and tomatoes like so many people do, but we have just the right spices to cook into the mix. Your mother knows the recipe even better than I do. She will share it with you some time. The third secret isn't as much of a secret, but it is just as important. Those cooking kettles I use out back are called Dutch ovens. They are specially made to sit in the burning wood and coals and cook the meat evenly. Being able to put hot coals on top, as well as underneath, makes it easier to make sure all the meat gets cooked the same. No matter what new inventions they contrive to cook, no one will ever be able to improve on meat cooked in a Dutch oven."

Dad smiled at his son. "Now, Joe, you know my secrets, the secrets half the men in Little Rock would like to steal from me. I trust you to keep them faithfully. Don't even tell your best friend what I told you."

"I promise, Dad," Joe said fervently.

"Now where were we in my war story from 1874?" Dad pondered. "Oh, yes, shots had been fired on April 21. Men continued to carry guns around Little Rock for the next three weeks, but meanwhile other groups were gathering in other parts of the state to take sides in the war. Shooting broke out in New Gascony, down by Pine Bluff, on April 30, and nine men were killed and twenty were wounded. On May 3, five more men were killed in a battle at Arkansas Post. The supporters of Mr. Brooks put a larger cannon on the lawn of the State House, the cannon that is still sitting there today, to threaten Mr. Baxter. Both sides were trying to ship more weapons into Little Rock on the Arkansas River, and a battle broke out on the river on May 8. That was by Palarm, up the river from here. Two hundred men fighting for Mr. Brooks fired on a boat bringing fighters and guns for Mr. Baxter's side. Half of Mr. Baxter's supporters on the boat were either killed or injured in that one fight. From what began as a political scuffle, we now had a real war on our hands, and no one seemed to know how to end the fighting.

"Meanwhile, both sides had friends and lawyers working in the nation's capital, Washington DC, trying to get the president or Congress to do something to end the fighting. At first, President Ulysses S. Grant said that the problem belonged in Arkansas and it was up to the people of Arkansas to fix it. Finally, the president changed his mind, whether because of the lawyers or because of the people in Arkansas getting killed, I don't know. Messages were sent back and forth, and finally, on May 15, President Grant declared that Elisha Baxter was the proper governor of Arkansas. Mr. Baxter returned to the State House on May 19, Mr. Brooks disbanded his forces, amnesty was declared so that no one would be punished for his actions during the fighting, and the war was over as quickly as that."

Joe was about to comment, but he once again heard the rustling behind the store, and he could see that his father had heard it too. This time Bill Maxwell did not cross the store as quickly as he could, but instead moved slowly and quietly. He reached the door, which he had left ajar after the last attempt to catch the spy, and noiselessly pushed it farther open. With a quick jump, he was at the side of a boy about Joe's age who appeared to be trying to remove a sample from one of the pots. Dad shook the young man's arm in anger until the boy looked up at him and cried out, "Uncle Bill!"

"Johnnie?" asked Dad, dropping the boy's arm.

"Cousin Johnnie?" echoed Joe, standing in the back doorway of the store.

As soon as his arm was released, Johnnie rushed across the small yard, repeating his well-practiced leap over the fence, and tore down the alley. Dad laughed so hard he had to sit down in the dirt of the yard.

"It's worse than I feared," he chortled. "My own brother is not only trying to steal my secret recipe, but he's sending his own son to spy on me."

"Imagine that," Joe said, relieved to see his father's good humor over the incident. "Dishonesty and strife right in our own family. Why," he added as his eyes met his father's and he offered Dad a wink, "I never heard of such a thing!"

The Brooks-Baxter War, which began April 15, 1874, and ended May 16 of the same year following President Grant's proclamation, was fought entirely within the state of Arkansas between supporters of the two would-be governors. Roughly 200 fighters were killed, and many more were injured, as hundreds of men on both sides took up arms to support one leader or the other. Later in 1874, Augustus Garland was elected governor of Arkansas, after Elisha Baxter declined the nomination of his party.

chapter 4

ARKANSAS TROOPS ON STANDBY: THE SPANISH-AMERICAN WAR

Danny Williams ran home from school, more excited than he had been in a long time. The date was Monday, May 16, 1898. Danny was in the eighth grade at the little school about a mile from his family farm, which in turn was about two miles from Jonesboro, Arkansas. Danny had a baby brother they called Buster and two young sisters: Sarah, who was six years old, and Gabby, who was four years old. Danny was big for his age. He looked like a grown man, six feet tall and very broad through the shoulders and chest. Danny's father, Andy, ran a sawmill, as well as the farm, on the outskirts of Jonesboro, but he often said that Danny was too young to work in the big timber just yet. Dad helped Danny find work at Mr. Harvey's feed store after school. Danny also helped out at the Harvey Livery Stables. He had learned to groom horses here as well as on the farm. Danny's mother, Martha, cared for the children and helped out on the farm as much as she could.

Today, Danny's teacher had talked about the war going on in Cuba. Danny became more and more excited as he listened to Mr. Long speak. Mr. Long was telling the class that Arkansas governor Daniel W. Jones was calling for volunteer companies from all over Arkansas to send to Cuba to help the country fight for its independence from Spain.

Danny wanted badly to go to Cuba. He thought it would be wonderful to help another country gain its freedom. He talked to Mr. Long about enlisting, but Mr. Long said he was too young—one had to be at least eighteen years old to enlist.

Mr. Long said that the United States had decided to become involved in Cuba's war for independence from Spain after an

American ship, the *Maine*, had exploded in a Cuban harbor. An investigation had determined that the ship had been blown up by a mine. On April 19, Congress had passed a joint resolution calling for war against Spain, and, two days later, American ships had begun a blockade to keep Spanish ships from reaching Cuba. Finally, on April 25, Spain and the United States had each declared war on the other.

President William McKinley had called for volunteers to train as soldiers to fight Spain. Theodore Roosevelt decided to leave his post as assistant secretary to the U.S. Navy to raise a cavalry regiment in Texas, Oklahoma, and New Mexico. He was recruiting an experienced group of cowboys, hunters, and miners that he knew from his days in the Wild West, as well as college students from northeastern schools eager for adventure. Because of the Western volunteers' rough existence all their lives, and because of the uniform they had adopted, they were known as the Rough Riders.

Danny longed to be a Rough Rider, or at least fight beside them. He had always wanted to participate in what his father called a "grand mission." All evening as Danny loaded feed for Mr. Harvey, he thought about the exciting adventure. By the time he came home, he had resolved to ask his parents for permission to join the army, even though he was nearly certain they would say no.

Danny's father and his hired men had been working in the fields all day. Mom had made a handy fieldworkers' lunch for them, a dish she had learned to make growing up in southern Arkansas. She cooked meat with corn meal, then wrapped the mixture in the husks from the corn. The combination, easy to carry out into the field and eat on the spot, was called a tamale. Mom had made more tamales that morning than the men had eaten for lunch, so she added the extras to the family supper, much to Danny's delight. He began to eat as soon as Dad finished giving thanks for the meal.

"Danny, why are you eating so fast?" laughed Dad as he watched Danny wolf down one tamale and start another.

"Oh, Dad," sighed Danny, "I worked hard at Mr. Harvey's."

Dad nodded, smiling, as he buttered a biscuit for himself. Mom was carrying the baby on her hip as she poured a cup of coffee for Dad.

"Uh, Dad?" ventured Danny. "What do you know about the war in Cuba and Theodore Roosevelt's Rough Riders?"

Dad took a sip of the steaming hot coffee before answering.

"Well, son, not much really. I heard about them some when I went into town. Mr. Davis at the hardware store talks about the war all the time. He says Roosevelt is training the Westerners to go with him to try and win independence for Cuba from Spain. He says they are a tough group and that if anybody can help Cuba, it will be Roosevelt and his boys."

"Well, Dad," Danny began, dreading the reaction to his next words, "I really want to join the Arkansas regiment that is going down there. Mr. Long was telling us that at least one regiment is going to muster out of Little Rock. I want to join that unit."

"What!" Dad yelled, almost choking on his biscuit. "Are you completely crazy? You know you are too young to join the army for any reason. You are only fifteen years old—you know nothing about fighting! I forbid it, I absolutely forbid it!" Dad shouted as he thumped his fist upon the table, his supper completely forgotten.

"But, Dad, listen to me," Danny begged, "I know what I am doing!"

"No, you don't!" Dad thundered. "You absolutely don't know what you are saying!"

Mom began crying, which made the baby cry. Dad rushed to Mom's side and said soothingly, "Now, Martha, you know I'm not going to let him do that. Go on and calm down the baby. Everything will be all right."

"Danny, please," begged Mom, "think about this. You know your dad is right. You are too young, and besides, we need you here."

"Martha," Dad soothed, "go quiet down the baby. It will be all right. I'll talk to the boy. Stop worrying."

Mom turned to leave the room, still crying. She looked back as she departed.

She said, "Danny, you can't do this—you are too young and it is too dangerous. Promise me you'll never mention this again. We could never get over losing you."

Danny was completely shocked. He never expected such a violent reaction from his parents. He thought they might say no, but he never expected them to yell and cry. Danny knew in his heart that they were both scared. They just didn't realize how strong he was. They just didn't want him to get hurt.

But Danny knew he wouldn't get hurt. This was his destiny. He had to devise a plan to sneak off to Little Rock and join the army regiment there. He knew he looked at least twenty years old, so he could enlist and lie about his age. Now he just had to figure out a way to slip away without his parents missing him. He lay awake that night, tossing and turning. As hard as he thought, though, no plan would come to him.

The week went by, and still no plan came to Danny. Mr. Long said that men from all over Arkansas were gathering in Little Rock to fight in the war against Spain. Danny wanted with all his heart to join them, even though he did not want to disobey his parents or hurt them.

Finally, by Friday, Danny had thought of a plan. His teacher, Mr. Long, kept two horses at Mr. Harvey's livery stables. One was a mare that Mr. Long had always wanted to breed to Danny's cousin Mike's Appaloosa stud horse. He would tell Mr. Long that he would take this mare to Mike, who lived near Jonesboro. Cousin Mike would shoe the horse for him, then breed her to his beautiful Appaloosa. Danny knew that Mr. Long would do this because he talked a lot about wanting an Appaloosa colt. Danny also knew that his father would let him do Mr. Long this favor, because Dad liked Mr. Long. Danny had already completed most of his school projects, so everyone should agree.

And the next day, they did. Dad hoped that this favor for Mr. Long would get his son's mind off joining the army. Danny packed a few clothes and picked up Mr. Long's chestnut bay mare at Mr. Harvey's livery stables early the next morning. He rode the horse into town and left her with his cousin. From there, he walked to the train station. Danny had scraped together his life's savings of nickels and dimes. He had fifty cents, just enough to ride the train to Little Rock. Once there, he asked directions to Camp Dodge, where the volunteer soldiers were gathering.

Just as Danny thought, nobody questioned his age. The first

group of volunteers had already been assembled, but a second regiment was set to be gathered starting on Wednesday, under the command of Virgil Y. Cook. Colonel Cook was especially glad to see Danny because many of his troops were failing the physical examination. A strapping young boy like Danny was very welcome to Cook's regiment. The colonel even allowed Danny to stay with him and eat with his family until Wednesday.

From May 25 through May 30, the volunteers forming Arkansas's Second Regiment gathered at Camp Dodge. They drilled every day, learning how to think

Colonel Elias Chandler led the first Arkansas regiment and lectured troops from both regiments while they trained at Camp Thomas in Georgia.
Photo courtesy of the Butler Center for Arkansas Studies.

as soldiers and how to use their weapons. They shot at targets, and they went on long marches. When Colonel Cook said that the group was ready, they left for Camp Thomas at Chickamauga Park. More than thirty years earlier, a Civil War battle had been fought at this place on the northern tip of Georgia, just south of Chattanooga, Tennessee. Here, the troops continued their training, and they also were told more about the war in which they were fighting.

Colonel Elias Chandler, who had led the first regiment from Arkansas, told the assembled troops about many cruel acts in Cuba that had enraged Americans for many years. In 1873, five years into a Cuban uprising, a Spanish warship captured the American steamer *Virginia* as it attempted to deliver guns, ammunition, and medical supplies to Cuban patriots. Some rebel leaders aboard the *Virginia* were shot and decapitated, their heads placed on pikes. Captain Joseph Frye and forty-eight of his crewmen were executed by a firing squad. Spain reluctantly released the survivors and paid a small amount of money. But this bloody incident was not forgotten by the United States.

In 1875, Spain responded to another Cuban revolt by sending General Valeriano Weyler to the island. He was called "Butcher Weyler" by the *New York Press*. His scorched-earth policy devastated eastern Cuba and led to the deaths of thousands of civilians. The Spanish seemed to be intent on breaking the Cuban people.

By 1897, Cuban rebels were appearing nightly in the traveling show Buffalo Bill Cody's Wild West Extravaganza as part of his Congress of Rough Riders of the World. The press exploited every Spanish atrocity, real or imagined. Colonel Chandler said that the American people fumed and fretted over Cuba. They believed the Cuban rebels were soul mates of the American revolutionaries of 1776.

The final straw was when the U.S. battleship *Maine* blew up in Havana harbor. Two hundred and sixty American sailors were dead. "Remember the *Maine!*" was the slogan cried in political speeches and newspaper articles. The result, as Mr. Long had told the class back in Jonesboro, was that the United States had blockaded Cuba and war had been declared.

The soldiers in training all listened quietly to Colonel Chandler's lectures night after night. When they had time to talk to each other, Danny learned that not every soldier believed what the colonel had been saying. One of Danny's new friends was especially skeptical. Paul Harper was from Harrison, another town in northern Arkansas. Like Danny, Paul had run away to join the army, but he had not joined because he wanted to fight. He joined the army because he did not want to be a railroad worker like his father. Whenever he had the chance, he would whisper to Danny, "You don't really believe all those things the colonel's telling us, do you?"

Of course Danny believed.

"Would we be fighting a war if the Spanish government hadn't done all these things?" Danny asked Paul.

"You bet we would fight. The Spanish were trying to stop

a part of their country from breaking away, and they didn't do anything that we wouldn't do if one of our states wanted to break away. If the Spanish attacked Americans, it probably means the Americans were looking for trouble."

"But what about the *Virginia*? And the *Maine*?" Danny could not believe that a man like Colonel Chandler would be less than fully honest with the soldiers.

"Aw, the *Maine* probably just had some sort of accident. Ships have explosions all the time, and hardly ever is it because of a mine or other bomb."

As the days went by, Danny and his regiment were still waiting in Camp Thomas. The conditions were terrible. Mosquitoes were everywhere, and sanitation was practically unknown. The food was nothing like what Danny had known on the farm. Never were the men served fresh fruit or vegetables, and the meat that had been sold to the army was old and in poor condition. Danny dreamed of eating just one of his mother's tamales, but when he described them to his fellow soldiers, many of them just laughed at him.

The men in the regiment were beginning to get sick. Poor living conditions and unsanitary food—along with the mosquitoes, ticks, flies, and lice—all took a toll on the men. Their bodies began to weaken. Many of the troops became deathly ill. An outbreak of smallpox also killed many of the Arkansas volunteers. Danny watched as many of his new friends and acquaintances became horribly sick.

Danny was really beginning to get homesick. He missed his mother's cooking and even longed for his old job back at Mr. Harvey's feed store and livery stables. He missed Mr. Long and the way he explained to the class what was happening in the world. Most of all, Danny sorely regretted deceiving his family. As the days went by, the only action Danny ever saw were people sick and dying. His own body was riddled with mosquito and tick bites, and he feared getting the fever with each passing day. The reports given by Colonel Chandler were the only thing Danny looked forward to.

Colonel Chandler often talked of the honorable moral fiber of Theodore Roosevelt. His Rough Rider group had left Florida on the thirteenth of June to fight in Cuba. By the first of July, they were fighting near the important city of Santiago. Two major hills needed to be taken, Kettle Hill and San Juan Hill. The Rough Riders had been assigned a position near the large American guns, but Roosevelt thought that they were in danger both from enemy fire and from their own barrage. He moved his men into the tall grass for cover and waited for the order to advance. No order was given. Roosevelt feared that the advantage of the Americans would be lost, so when no superior officer was near, Roosevelt gave the order to charge. Remaining on horseback so he could see his men, he directed them up Kettle Hill. The volunteers hesitated at first, then followed his direction and charged. Kettle Hill was won.

The colonel's description of the next attack was even more dramatic. Once again, Roosevelt found his men easy targets for enemy fire, so he called for a charge up San Juan Hill. After about a hundred-yard sprint, he looked around and noticed that only five of his men had joined him. One of the men was fatally shot and another was wounded as bullets flew around them. Roosevelt realized that the rest of his men had not heard his command and went back to get them. Again he ordered the charge, and this time the hill was captured. The Americans won the day. After San Juan Hill, the city of Santiago was easily taken, and the Rough Riders were headed for glory.

Danny's friend Paul was in the infirmary with a severe fever and missed Colonel Chandler's report. Danny visited his friend and repeated what the colonel had said. Paul rolled his eyes ironically as he listened to the tales of heroics from Cuba, but either he did not care to dampen Danny's spirits or he felt too weak to argue. Repeating the news of the Rough Riders was the last conversation Danny had with his friend. The next morning he learned that Paul had died during the night.

Just a few days after Paul's death, Danny and his Arkansas regiment were told that they were leaving for Puerto Rico. They prepared their supplies and were ready for the trip, but their orders were rescinded after two days. Spain, they were told, had accepted an American proposal to end the war. Spain would lose control of Cuba, the Philippines, and other islands in the Caribbean Sea and in the Pacific Ocean, but the war would be over.

A month later, the Second Regiment from Arkansas left Camp Thomas and was transferred to Camp Shipp in Alabama. They continued to train there, as some of the men hoped for careers in the army and others expected to fight in the Philippines if the negotiations with Spain did not succeed. Danny just wanted to go home. He had begun writing letters to his parents from Camp Thomas, and he continued to write to them from Camp Shipp. Finally, on February 25, 1899, the regiment was mustered out and Danny was permitted to return home.

When Danny arrived in Jonesboro, he had just turned sixteen years old. He was thin and weak from lack of food. His body was covered with infected sores. He dreaded facing his mother and father, wondering what they would say to him about the way he had run away from home.

To Danny's surprise, his father was waiting for him at the train station. As Danny stepped off the train, his father ran to him and wrapped his arms around him.

"Father," Danny began, "I'm so sorry. I know that what I did was wrong. I don't even deserve to be part of the family anymore."

"Of course you are part of the family!" his father exclaimed. "As soon as we got your letter telling us when you would be home, your mother started cooking. Tomorrow we're having a big party with all the neighbors, but tonight it will be just the family. And guess what? Your mother is making your favorite food, and you must remember what that is..."

Danny's face broke into a huge grin as he exclaimed, "Tamales!"

The United States and Spain declared war on each other on April 25, 1898. Battles were fought in Cuba, Puerto Rico, and the Philippines during the next few months. By the end of July, the governments were negotiating a peace treaty, which was eventually signed on December 10, ending Spanish control of many of its former possessions. The United States had slightly more than 300,000 soldiers in its armed forces during the months of the conflict, many of whom had volunteered for service because of the war with Spain. During the war, 385 Americans died in battle and 1,662 were injured. An additional 2,061 American soldiers died of illnesses during the war. Spanish losses in the war are estimated at between 55,000 and 60,000, with more than ninety percent dying from illnesses rather than in battle. About 2,000 Arkansans volunteered to fight in the war with Spain. Fifty-four died of illness, but none were killed or injured in battle. The cause of the explosion on the Maine is still uncertain today.

chapter 5

THE GREAT WAR, FREEDOM, AND ARKANSAS: WORLD WAR I

The sweat trickled down thirteen-year-old Lucy May Borden's back as she slowly worked her way down the last row of cotton for the day. Insects buzzed around her. They aggravated her already irritated eyes, which were swollen from allergies and from crying the night before. Lucy May belonged to a family of black sharecroppers in Desha County, Arkansas. They sharecropped for Judge Roscoe Jenkins on a farm a couple of miles from the town of Dumas. Sharecropping meant that the land was owned by Judge Jenkins, and Lucy May's family worked the judge's land. Papa and Judge Jenkins split the profits after all the expenses had been paid.

Lucy May did not often cry, but she had good reason to cry on this occasion. Last night, the Borden family had just sat down to supper. Papa had been given a few fresh-caught catfish, which Mama had cooked and served with cornbread muffins and mixed greens. The family had been laughing and talking when, suddenly, a brick came sailing through the window, barely missing Lucy May's head before it landed in the middle of the table, shattering a couple of plates and breaking two glasses of milk.

No one said a word for a few seconds. Then Papa jumped to his feet, throwing his chair backward with an awful thump. The baby began to scream. Mama and Lucy May tried to comfort the baby as Papa ran out the door. Then they all saw the hooded figures sitting on horses prancing back and forth, holding flaming torches in their hands.

"Elisha Borden!" thundered one of the hooded figures. "You better watch your mouth come Sunday morning. We hear you are telling your congregation that they should be voting in more elections. I hear that you even offered to pay the poll tax for some of them!"

Papa stood still, his shoulders straight and his head high. He stared straight ahead. He did not answer the hooded figures.

"You hear me, Elisha Borden?" screamed the hooded figure again. "Don't you just stand there and ignore me. You better mind what I say, boy—next time, it will be worse!" With that, the hooded man touched his torch to Mama's feathers and corn husks hanging from the barn rafters. They immediately began to burn. The hooded figures rode off laughing.

The leader stopped and looked back at Papa and said, "The next time it will be your house, boy. Now mind your words. We don't need any of that Bolshevism you brought back with you from Europe in our fields." With the bark of a laugh, he turned his horse and whipped it to a gallop to catch up to the others.

Lucy May and Mama were crying, running alongside Papa to get water from the well to put out the fire. Mama carried the howling baby. They knew that if the fire spread, the whole barn would ignite, and all the crops would burn. They might even lose the house. They drew buckets of water from the well and doused the flames, finally putting the fire out after two hours of hard work. Some of the exposed rafters burned, but the main structure was safe.

Lucy May was exhausted after the fire was put out. She felt weak and helpless. She helped her mother clean up the mess in the kitchen, trembling and crying. This was the third time in the last six months that her father had been threatened, but it was the first time anyone had tried to hurt the family. Lucy May feared for his life. As a matter of fact, Lucy May thought the hooded figures might be people that they knew, though she couldn't quite place them. Lucy May finally went to bed, but she could not sleep. She tossed and turned. She heard Mama and Papa talking in the next room. Their voices were low, but she knew that they were more upset than they seemed.

Lucy May's father, the Reverend Elisha Borden, had never been satisfied with the sharecropping system. He was sure that the judge was cheating them every year. Papa never made much more than $100 a year over expenses, and he knew he should get much more than that. But Papa had been taught only enough to read his Bible. He always had to work in the fields and hardly ever went to school. He had never learned any of the skills of "figuring." He couldn't prove how much the judge was actually cheating him.

It was the end of September 1919, and the cotton was being brought in from the fields. No school was held while cotton remained to be picked. Everyone who could walk moved up and down the rows of cotton, patiently pulling the white fluff from the dried stalks and dropping it into the bags that hung at their sides and—for all but the tallest men—dragged on the ground behind them. On other farms, the full bags were weighed, and workers received a promise of money according to the weight of the cotton they had picked. Usually that promise of money was good for credit at the local store, which also was owned by the judge. Because Papa was a sharecropper, however, his labor and that of his family were not counted for wages. The work was expected, from Papa and Mama and from any children who were big enough to carry a bag. The profits from the land would be divided later, when the crop had been sold at market.

Lucy May had two younger brothers, ten-year-old Levi and Jake, who was three months old. Levi worked as fast as he could, hoping to fill as many bags as a full-grown man. Jake rode in a sack on his mother's back, although sometimes Lucy May wore him on her back. Mama worked in the fields with the rest of the family, when she wasn't busy preparing food for the rest of them to eat. Mama did all she could to save the family money. She patched their old clothes, sometimes shortening Papa's pants so Levi could wear them. She saved the feathers from the chickens to make feather beds and feather pillows for her family. She and the children had also shelled a bushel of popcorn throughout the weeknights. A parishioner had given the popcorn to Papa last Sunday. Mama saved the corn husks because she made dolls for the kids with them if she had a little time to spare.

Finally, the long, hot day was over. Lucy May stopped by the spring on her way home. The clear, cool water was refreshing, and she began to feel a little better. She ran up the steps of the house just in time to hear her Mama say, "I'm scared this time,

Elisha. I want to send Lucy May to my sister up by Elaine. I wish all the children could go, but you need me here, and Jake needs me, and Levi might still be some help. Lucy May we can spare. If we get her out of here, at least one of the family will be safe from their threats."

Papa just sat there, not saying a word. His head was bowed, and he seemed to have aged ten years overnight. Finally, he looked up at Mama. Lucy May thought she could see tears shining on his face. He just nodded and slowly walked out the back door toward the garden.

Mama looked up and said, "Well, I guess you heard us talking, honey. I believe you will be safer with Aunt Eliza and Uncle John. The rest of us will join you soon, I hope."

Lucy May was shocked. Never in her wildest dreams did she think anything could split the family apart. The whole family had been up to Aunt Liza's once or twice a year as long as Lucy May could remember, but never had just one of them spent the night, let alone several days and nights without any plan for when to return.

After supper that Friday, Papa hitched the horse to the wagon. Lucy May climbed on the seat next to him. She had no baggage to bring with her for the trip—nothing but the clothes she was wearing and two favorite cornhusk dolls she had tucked into the pocket of her apron. At first Papa was silent as they began their trip in the deepening dusk. Then he shook his head and said, in his low, soft voice, "I never thought I would have to run away from any man. After we've gone and fought for our country, seems to me we should be treated the same as anyone else. Yet the cotton sells for more money now than it did before the war, and somehow we don't get paid any more." After a few more minutes of silence, he added, "They told us we were going over there to fight for freedom. Seems that after we fought and bled and some of us died, we ought to have a bit of freedom back here."

Lucy May remembered the fifteen months her father had been away from home, fighting in the Great War somewhere across the ocean. Reaching out in the dark, she touched her father's arm and asked, "Papa? Were you frightened when you were over there fighting in that war?"

Papa grunted at first, as if he had forgotten that he was not alone in the wagon. Then he said, "Child, I was more frightened being trained to fight than I ever was in France. When they first made us register for the draft, I didn't think they'd take a dark-skinned farm worker like me. I was shocked when they told me to report to Camp Pike, up north of Little Rock. I'd never been so far away from home in all my life, and I was surrounded by strangers from all over Arkansas, away from home for the first time, just like me."

"They had two camps, of course: one for the white trainees and one for the black trainees. I was one of the first black men sent there. When I first arrived, I was so excited. I loved the camp. I could go to the city every Saturday if I wanted to. I went to picture shows, which I had never seen before. The training was rough but not unreasonable at first. I even saved a little money."

Lucy May cuddled up next her father and waited for the story to continue. His voice began to falter as he traveled deeper into his memories.

"Scripture says that the imagination of a man's heart is evil from his youth, and whoever thought up this war business must have the most evil imagination of all. They taught us to fire guns at that camp and tried to make us believe that shooting a soldier on the other side is nothing more than shooting a wild animal, a bear or a wildcat. Worse than that, they told us that the Germans would be shooting the same way at us, hunting us down like animals. They taught us how to hide in trenches, how to keep from being shot. They told us that when a man shoots in your direction, you have to hold real still, to make him think you aren't there. We had to learn how to keep still, even when we were frightened and wanted to run away, because the ones who get up to run away are generally the ones that get shot and killed."

Lucy May remembered what it had been like for her during the war, sitting with the women and the other older girls, preparing bandages for the Red Cross to send to the troops in France. With every bandage they rolled, Lucy May prayed for the soldier that it would help, and she also prayed that her father would never need a bandage like the ones she was helping to prepare.

"Then they told us the rest of it, that the war had more than guns. They told us about bombs that drop from the sky and tear apart whatever is near when they fall. They told us about bombs called mines that are buried in the ground so they blow up whoever steps on them. They told us about poisons that creep along the ground and tear up a man from the inside. Before they sent us to France, they gave us each a gas mask to wear, with big eyes and a long nose, something like an elephant's face. We laughed when we first saw it, but we didn't laugh when they told us what happened to the men who didn't wear their gas masks."

Papa shuddered, and Lucy May shuddered with him. As the ride continued, stars began to sparkle in the sky. A dim crescent moon gradually shone brighter in the western sky. Papa's voice remained low and sad.

"We got to London and saw what the bombs had been doing. I saw blocks of houses reduced to stone and ashes. I saw a castle a thousand years old that had been destroyed by a modern bomb. I saw people living in fear, rushing for shelter every time the sirens warned of another bomb attack. Then we got to France, and I saw the trenches where we had to hide and shoot. I saw the stumps of trees, already torn apart by bombs. I saw the bodies of men who breathed in the poison gas and died. I saw the bodies of men who got scared and jumped up and ran and got shot and died. I held the hand of one man as he lay dying, shot in the chest by some stranger in another trench." Papa's voice choked and he remained quiet for a few minutes. Lucy May snuggled close enough to hear his heart thump, even louder than the sound of the horse's feet on the dirt road.

Finally, Papa added, "All that time, I reminded myself why I was there. I was fighting to protect you and your brother and your mother. I was making sure you could be free and safe. Even if I died over there, I thought it would be all right, because the three of you would live on in a better world, a world without fear and without war and without danger."

They traveled on in silence until they reached the home of Uncle John and Aunt Liza. Explanations were quickly made and accepted, and Papa turned the horse and wagon around to head back home. Uncle John invited him to stay the night, but they both knew Papa couldn't. Cotton had to be picked, even on Saturday, and Papa also needed time to study the scriptures by candlelight so he had a message to preach Sunday morning.

When day dawned, Lucy May was introduced to Beth Clark, the girl who lived next door. Beth was twelve and was eager to show Lucy her house and farm, a cotton farm just like Lucy May's home. A drainage ditch, dry this time of year, marked the border between the two properties. A line of trees and tall bushes ran along the Clarks' side of the ditch. Lucy May and Beth found a flat patch of sand in the ditch where they could play with the dolls Lucy May had brought from home. The girls shared stories of their lives on the two similar farms. Lucy May boasted about her father, the soldier who had fought in the Great War. Beth told how her father had worked a few months in Helena at a factory that made wooden stocks for the guns that had been used in the war. They began the day as strangers and ended it as friends.

Sunday was odd, going to church with Uncle John and Aunt Liza, listening to someone other than her father preach. Lucy May wondered what her father was saying that Sunday. Would he have the courage to speak his mind, or would the threats of those men keep Papa from saying what was in his heart? If he preached what he felt was true, would they make good on their threats? Would they burn down the house? Would they try to hurt Papa?

With these questions on her mind, Monday and Tuesday were long days for Lucy May. She tried to comfort herself with the thought that, if anything bad had happened, word would spread, but hearing nothing from home was almost as frightening as hearing bad news. Lucy May reminded herself that her father had needed to be brave in France, and now she needed to be brave and do the right thing, no matter how hard it seemed.

Tuesday night after supper, Uncle John left the house.

"He's going off to a meeting for farmers," Aunt Liza told Lucy May. "You go to bed; I'll just sit here and wait up for him."

Lucy May lay in bed, staring up at the ceiling for what seemed like hours, but finally she fell asleep. In the morning, Aunt Liza was still sitting in the rocking chair. She tried to hide her worry, but Lucy May could see it in her face.

"Stay close to the house, girl," she said. "Something feels wrong about this day. Don't you go anywhere that you can't get back inside the house in a minute or less."

No one came to the house all day long, but Aunt Liza and Lucy May both heard sounds in the distance that sounded like gunfire. More than once they heard voices from the road that sounded like men shouting together or maybe singing. Lucy May stayed behind the house, on the other side of the road where she could not be seen, and played quietly with her dolls. She wished that Beth would come across the ditch to join her, but she supposed that Beth's mother was also keeping her close to the house.

Evening came, and Aunt Liza was stirring a pot of weak soup when a neighbor came to the back of the house and tapped quietly on the door.

"Mary!" Aunt Liza exclaimed, and let her in.

"It's terrible, Liza!" Mary gasped. "I can only stay for a minute, but I had to let you know. There's been trouble. There was shooting at the church last night, and, all day long, men have been coming into town with guns and shooting at any of us they see. Some of the men are even soldiers wearing uniforms. Now, I know your John is alive, but he's locked up in the jail, and we don't know how safe he'll be there. We don't know how safe any of us is. If you can, tonight or tomorrow, get word to the Clarks down the road. I don't dare try to go there, and I wouldn't bother you with it, but Ezra's in the jail same as John, and I don't think Sarah knows." The women cried together briefly, and then Mary left quietly out the back door.

It took Lucy May a minute to find her voice, but then she said to her aunt, "Please let me go to the Clarks. They need to know, and I'm sure I can get there and back safer than you."

"Oh, girl, your parents sent you here to keep you safe. You know I can't let you go out at a time like this. Don't even think of it!"

"Aunt Liza, I'll lose my mind sitting here in the house, not being of any use to anyone. Please let me go. Miss Sarah is probably wondering, just like you were wondering about Uncle John. She needs to be told, just like Miss Mary told you. Please, Aunt Liza, I know my way there, I promise I'll be safe." Lucy May knew that Beth also would be wondering about her father and worried, and she longed to see her new friend and assure her that, even if he was in danger, her father was still alive.

A little more arguing, and Lucy May was on her way. Slipping through the shadows, she made her way to the line of trees that separated the two farms. Carefully she wound her way to the house and knocked on the back door, quietly as Mary had done. She delivered the message breathlessly, using almost the same words Mary had done, as best as Lucy May could remember them. "There's been trouble in the town. Uncle John and your husband Ezra are both locked up in the jail. They haven't been hurt, but Miss Mary is scared; she doesn't know how long they'll be safe there."

Sarah and Beth were speechless at first. Then Sarah spoke her mind. "I told Ezra not to go to that meeting. I told him nothing good could come out of looking for more money for his work. The war is over, and everything has to be the way it was before we had the war. Why do the men think they have to get together and talk and make the landowners think bad things about them? Why can't they just accept the way things are?"

"Papa says the war was fought to keep us free," Lucy May answered. "Papa says this was the war to end all wars, the war to make all people free. He says that nothing is wrong in saying that every man should be paid fairly for his work."

"Child, keep quiet or you're going to bring the trouble right into our house. We don't need to talk about getting more money; we need to pray about keeping safe. Pray, child—pray for your uncle and for my Ezra. Pray that nothing bad will happen to them in that jail."

Lucy May did pray with Beth and with her mother. Then she reminded them, "Aunt Liza will be worried about me. I need to get back to her."

"Be careful, child. Get back to your aunt, and get back safe." Lucy May gave Sarah a hug, and then gave Beth a tighter hug. She could see the worry in her friend's eyes, and she knew that Beth was thinking not only about the men in jail but also about the commotion that had been heard through the day. What kind of things had been happening in their quiet part of the world?

Lucy May embraced Beth one more time and then slipped out the back door.

After crossing through the vegetable path, Lucy May ran among the stalks of cotton plants that already had been harvested. Soon she reached the drainage ditch and found herself on the patch of sand where, a few days before, she and Beth had played with the dolls. A little bit out of breath after her run, Lucy was starting to sit down to rest near a clump of bushes when she saw the man standing on the road. It was too dark to see whether he was wearing a uniform, but it was easy to see that he was carrying a gun.

Lucy May held her breath and tried to stay hidden in the bushes. Peering between the branches, she could see him facing her direction, gun aimed her way. The shot rang out in the night, and she heard the bullet fly past her. A scream began in her throat, but she held it inside her. She remembered her father's words from a few nights before: "We had to learn how to keep still, even when we were frightened and wanted to run away, because the ones who get up to run away are generally the ones that get shot and killed." Hard as it was, she forced her legs to keep still. A second shot was fired, not coming as near her as the first. In the still night, without even the sound of birds or frogs, she could hear the gun emptied of its cartridges and reloaded. She peered through the branches. The man stood, looking her direction, but no longer aiming his gun. After a minute or two more, he turned and started walking up the road toward town.

Lucy May exhaled, but other than that, she still did not move. First she counted to two hundred, then she dared to move along the trees back to Aunt Liza's home. The last stretch, across the cotton field, seemed the longest, but soon she had made it to the back door. "I'm back," she whispered as she edged into the house.

"Oh, girl, I was so frightened for you," exclaimed Aunt Liza, and the two fell into each other's arms and wept.

News continued to be passed from farm to farm, from back door to back door, over the following days. Most of the news was little more than rumor. Troops were coming from Camp Pike, and they had a machine gun, one of the terrible weapons that had been used in the war. Even the governor was coming from Little

Rock to end the fighting. Army troops were shooting at black men, whether alone or in groups. Black men were marching in formation and seeking to defend their homes and their families. No one was sure what to believe, and so the women and children stayed in their houses, eating what scraps of food they had left in their kitchens.

One week after they had last seen Uncle John, a piece of paper was brought to the house. It was delivered by a white soldier wearing an army uniform. Lucy May read it to Aunt Liza. "To the Negroes of Phillips County: The trouble at Hoop Spur and Elaine has been settled. Soldiers now here to preserve order will return to Little Rock within a short time. No innocent Negro has been arrested, and those of you who are at home and at work have no occasion to worry. All you have to do is remain at work just as if nothing had happened. Phillips County has always been a peaceful, law-abiding community, and normal conditions must be restored right away. Stop talking! Stay at home! Go to work! Don't worry!"

Late that evening, the sound of a horse in the yard sent Lucy May's heart up into her throat. A minute later, though, she heard the voice of her father calling loudly, "Liza! Are you at home? Is my little girl safe?" Lucy May ran to her father and gave him a big hug. In a matter of a few minutes, news was exchanged: Papa heard about Uncle John in jail, and Lucy May and her aunt learned that no trouble had yet hit the house near Dumas. "I've come to bring my daughter back home," Papa said. "You are welcome to join us if you wish."

Aunt Liza thought for a long time before she slowly answered, "No, Elisha, my place is near my man as long as there is hope. I surely appreciate your offer, and I know you mean it, but as long as I know John is alive, I need to stay near where he is."

Lucy May rode home with her father and told him about the shooting in the dark. She could not see his face as he spoke, but she could hear the mix of emotions in his voice as he said to her, "Little girl, I am proud of you." Pride was in his voice, but so were worry and fear.

That Sunday, Elisha Borden told the congregation, "This is my last day to stand before you and speak to you. For the good of my family, I am taking them out of this place. I will go to Pine

Bluff to look for work. If no jobs are available there, I will go to Little Rock, then to St. Louis, then maybe to Chicago or Detroit. I will continue seeking until I find a place where we can be safe, where my little children can grow up without fear or danger." He stopped for a minute, and then said to the people who had gathered to hear him, "I never thought I would be leaving the land where I was born, but they sent me to France to fight for freedom. Now, again, I fight for freedom, for myself and for my family. God bless you all."

World War I, referred to at the time as the Great War, was mostly fought in Europe, although it also included battles in Africa and Asia, as well as battles at sea. Triggered on June 28, 1914, by an assassination in Sarajevo, it ended on November 11, 1918, with an armistice that led to the Treaty of Versailles the following year. Fifteen countries sent roughly 65 million soldiers into the conflict, of whom 8.5 million were killed, 21 million were injured, and 7.7 million were captured or went missing. The United States did not enter the war until April 6, 1917, but it sent 4.3 million soldiers to fight in Europe; 126,000 were killed, 234,000 were injured, and 4,500 were captured or went missing. In Arkansas, 149,027 were registered for possible service on June 5, 1917. When the draft age was raised the following year, a total of 199,857 men in Arkansas were listed as eligible to serve. Ultimately, 71,862 Arkansans entered the U.S. armed forces, of whom 2,183 died (more than half of illness or accidents before leaving the country) and 1,751 were wounded.

The Elaine Massacre began with gunshots outside a church in Hoop Spur, Arkansas, late in the night of September 30, 1919; black farmers were meeting in the church to discuss organizing so they could be paid better prices for their cotton and other crops. No one knows who fired the first shots at Hoop Spur. Between 600 and 1,000 white residents of Phillips County and the surrounding region gathered to fight what they claimed was an uprising by their black neighbors. Five hundred troops arrived from Camp Pike on October 2, officially to restore peace to the area, although some witnesses say that they joined in the shooting of black citizens. During these three days, five white citizens died and a large number of black citizens were shot to death— estimates generally say that several hundred died. Nearly 300 black men were arrested and charged with murder or other crimes; many of them were never tried. Twelve were sentenced to death, but they were eventually released after years of court cases; dozens more were sentenced to prison terms. No white people were ever arrested or charged for any event related to the massacre.

In January 1946, Private Thurlow Branscum received an honorable discharge from the United States army. These discharge papers show that for his service to his country he received seven decorations and commendations, including two Bronze Stars.

Papers reproduced courtesy of Velma B. Branscum Woody.

chapter 6

PAINFUL MEMORIES: WORLD WAR II

The day was June 21, 1960. Berniece Branscum sat on a blanket on the bank of a bubbling stream. The air was warm, but the gentle breeze through the many oak trees at the edge of the water made the beautiful day comfortable. Today was Berniece's twelfth birthday.

Berniece's father and mother, Thurlow and Mamie Branscum, were catching small fish called bumpy suckers for her birthday dinner. Berniece loved eating on the creek bank. She always wanted a "camp-out" for her birthday. Dad hunted a few quail for the event, and Mom prepared the quail along with the fish, right by the bubbling stream. When they returned with the fish, her mother built a natural stove from flat rocks she found near the creek. She placed one thick stone in the ground on its side and then another about a foot from the first. She then placed an old wire rack on the two stones, building a fire from driftwood found on the shore. She baked potatoes in the coals of the fire and made a salad from fresh garden vegetables she had brought from the farm, including the first tomatoes of the year. Mom had baked the birthday cake at home.

Soon Mama said, "Come on honey—it's ready."

Her parents began to sing "Happy Birthday," she made a wish and blew out the twelve candles, and they began to eat.

After the birthday meal, Berniece snuggled close to her father. She asked him if he would tell her of the years he spent in the army fighting in World War II. Dad didn't talk about those years very much. They seemed to make him sad.

Her mother said, "I believe I'll go look for some sweet gum. I think I know where I can find a sweet gum tree. It will be an extra treat for your birthday, honey." Sweet gum trees usually

Private Thurlow Branscum served in the Philippine Islands and other parts of the Pacific Ocean during World War II. Fifteen years later, on a family picnic, he shared his memories of the war with his daughter, Berniece. Photo courtesy of Velma B. Branscum Woody.

grew around a creek. The rosin under the bark could be chewed like bubblegum and was somewhat minty; gum was a special treat not often allowed. Berniece also knew that Mom wanted to find something to do so she wouldn't have to remember the most dreadful years of her life. Berniece had not lived through those years. She was born after Dad's return home.

Dad watched Mom walk away. He said, "Honey, the war years were horrible for your mother. It broke her heart when I was drafted. She was scared to death that I would die in action. She just doesn't want to remember anything or hear anything that happened while I was away."

"I know, Daddy," Berniece answered. "She told me she rode Old Ball, her horse, four or five miles each day to the post office to get a letter from you. She said she stayed with Grandpa Charlie, Grandma Emmer, and Uncle Bunion. She worked like a man beside them here on the farm all the time you were gone."

"She did, Sis. I would have never been able to buy this place if your mom hadn't worked so hard and managed the money I sent so well. She was really good to my family, and they love her like a daughter and sister. When I returned, she had saved most of my war wages. We bought this farm, which has been very good to us."

"I know, Daddy, I know," Berniece spoke somewhat impatiently. "But I want to hear about your days in World War II."

"Well, okay," sighed Daddy.

Daddy began to talk. His memory went back to the end of 1942 when he was drafted by the U.S. Army.

"My brother, Bunion, and I had received a draft notice. We were sent to Little Rock for a physical. Bunion failed the physical because of an old knee injury, but I passed. Before I knew it, I was on a train headed for the army training camp called Camp Chaffee, not far from Fort Smith. After the training, I was sent to North Carolina. This camp was located in and around huge pine trees that moaned like lonesome bagpipes in the wind. My sergeant was very tough. He yelled and screamed at us and made us feel as if we could do nothing right. He began toughening the men of his regiment, though some of the men began to break. I knew a man who ran. He was actually in my battalion and bunked close to me. He just suddenly disappeared. He seemed all right, but then he was missing. Three days later, he was found, shaking and trembling and crying. I always had this thought in the back of my mind: 'There but for the grace of God go I.'

"One day, our regiment was training 'under the gun.' We were crawling on the ground, and our officers were shooting over our heads with real bullets. They told us to not stand up no matter what happened. We were crawling along as bullets whizzed over our heads. Suddenly, one guy broke. He stood up and started running as fast as he could. The bullets caught him. He died before he hit the ground. I guess I trained out pretty good because I was assigned to 81st Infantry 'Wildcat' Division. We were the 'sharp shooters,' meaning that we were the best shots in the army. If we aimed at a target, we would usually hit it. We were often the ones who used the flame throwers. I had to learn to say, '38-357-748, private first class, Company B, 52nd Engineer Combat Battalion.' I have never forgotten this. I never will. It was a label that never left my mind."

"Why did you have to learn to say those words?" Berniece asked her father, snuggling closer to him and draping his arm across her shoulders.

"The main reason was that, if any of us were captured by the enemy, all we were supposed to tell them was our 'name, rank, and serial number.' The army leaders knew that anything else we might say, however innocent it seemed to us, might in some way be used against us or against the army as a whole. To make sure that we would be in the habit of saying our rank and serial number without adding anything, we were required to identify ourselves that way everywhere we went as part of the army.

"We usually fought in the Philippine Islands, but our Wildcats were once sent to Okinawa. Myself and a few others who were known as marksmen had been chosen to take flame throwers into the caves. Now, this was not an easy task. The whole island was riddled with caves and tunnels often joining each other. Sometimes, a whole group of Japanese soldiers would hide in one of these caves. They would have food and water, enough to supply them for weeks. When the Americans would move near or camp by one of their 'holes,' their snipers would pick us off one by one."

Berniece shuddered, considering how easy it would have been for her father to have been one of the victims of those snipers. Why, he might never have returned to Arkansas, and she might never even have been born.

"Even though our Wildcats were considered one of the army's best units," he continued, "we still had our job cut out for us when we went into the elaborate cave system with the flame throwers. But this was the only way we could get the Japanese soldiers out. It was horrible. But war is a very horrible business.

"One day, I was walking through the jungles of Okinawa. The broad jungle leaves were heavy with moisture. The drops fell on my helmet as I waded knee-deep in the jungle mud. Now, we had been warned about snakes falling on our heads, and we had to be on constant lookout for snipers. I never encountered a falling snake, but I found several snipers. We knew approximately where some of the caves were located, but we didn't know where they all were. Suddenly, out of nowhere, a shot rang out. The bullet whizzed by my ear, and I hit the ground, shooting from my hip as I went down. I heard a scream then, words that were not English coming from somewhere near me. I cautiously came to my feet. I looked around trying to find the sound. Suddenly, I stumbled on something. I looked down and saw a young man lying at my feet. He couldn't have been more than seventeen years old. I was astonished. I raised the bayonet to strike but was touched by his sobbing. He didn't beg for mercy, but his sobs were heartbreaking. I acted as if I heard something behind me and made a quick exit. I often wondered if my show of mercy hurt others. I'd like to think that the young man survived and lived a better life because of my mercy. But I'll never know for sure."

Her father paused, thinking back to the events that he had tried to forget for the past fifteen years. Berniece heard the sounds of the river water lapping at the banks. She heard cicadas singing in the treetops. She watched as a pair of squirrels chased each other up and down the trunks of the larger trees. Finally, her father continued speaking.

"When I was in the Philippine Islands, it was nothing for a group of us to unload dead bodies in gunny sacks all night long. Bulldozers prepared ditches in which we threw the dead bodies. Many Americans were killed, too many for the bodies to be returned home. We could be walking in the rice paddies and see a man's leg floating by. It was nothing to see body parts floating around in the rice paddies. The war was wearing everybody down. We saw things too horrible to tell anybody.

"As the days wore on and we came closer to the end of the war, reports on the radio kept us knowledgeable of what was happening in other parts of the world. The war effort had a character they called Kilroy. He was used as a morale booster, mostly on radio, as a diversion from the horrible, depressing conditions of war. Kilroy was amazing. He was everywhere, anywhere, and always the first to arrive. No matter where we were, Kilroy was there, too. Soldiers drove Japanese troops out of a mountainside cave, and when they cautiously entered, they saw the familiar writing on the wall, 'Kilroy was here.' The writing appeared on the Marco Polo Bridge in China, the Tomb of the Unknown Soldier in Paris, on packing boxes, and the walls of buildings on every continent. The antics of Kilroy always made the soldiers laugh. It was a relief from the drudgery of war."

"So who was Kilroy? Was he a real soldier?" Berniece asked.

"Maybe once there was a real soldier named Kilroy who started the whole thing. I don't know. By the time I was in the army, Kilroy was a symbol who represented all of us. Any of us could be Kilroy. I think all of us thought of ourselves as Kilroy, or as his best friend or his little brother. All of us felt better knowing that Kilroy was fighting along with us and that he was just like us."

The two squirrels were on the same large oak, not far from Berniece and her father. The one being chased had frozen in place, its tail flat against the trunk, its head sticking out like the stub of a branch that had broken off the tree. The second squirrel was on the other side of the trunk. Whenever the second squirrel tried to move around the tree toward the first squirrel, that first squirrel would move just as far, keeping the tree between them. Berniece wondered if her father was watching the squirrels and if they reminded him of being in the war, hiding from the enemy, and trying to catch the enemy who was hiding.

"Your Mama wrote letters every day. Sometimes, I would get five in one day, and sometimes I wouldn't get one for a month. The mail was sporadic. Also, there were censors who would cross out anything in her letters that might give away information that would help the other side if the letter fell into their hands. My letters to her were censored even more strictly. Some things your Mama told me were things I already knew. Life was not easy back here in Arkansas either. Because so much was going into the war, people could not get a lot of things back here. Gasoline was strictly rationed. Sugar and meat and other foods were rationed too. New cars were not being made because all the factories were making cars or tanks or weapons for the war. New factories were built, including several in Arkansas; they did nothing but make weapons, or parts of weapons, for the war. Your aunt, your Mama's sister Alice, went to Jacksonville to work in the plant that was making fuses for bombs.

"People in Arkansas and in the other states collected anything that might be needed for war materiel: metal, rubber, and even paper. They prepared bandages for the Red Cross and donated blood to help soldiers who had been hurt. They gathered in churches and prayed for the soldiers; a lot of churches had special flags with stars for every soldier in the church—a white star if he was living and fighting in the war, and a gold star if he had died. Mama told me later that she prayed every night that she wouldn't have to sew a gold star on the church flag for me."

Again, Berniece shivered, even though the afternoon was warm. The thought that her father might have died in the war seemed very real to her. Suddenly she realized that many men had died, and that girls and boys like her probably had never been born because some soldiers had not lived long enough to be their fathers.

"Some things your mother did not write to me, but I learned them after the war was over. In addition to Camp Robinson near Little Rock and Camp Chaffee near Fort Smith, several air fields were built in Arkansas where people learned how to fly planes for the Army Air Force. Also, Arkansas had two camps where Japanese people—most of them American citizens—were interned during the war, because our government feared that they might help the enemy. German and Italian prisoners of war also were kept in Arkansas. They were housed at three large camps and at several smaller camps where they could be borrowed to help work the fields, replacing farmers who were fighting in the war. Camp Robinson was the model POW camp in Arkansas. It included barracks, housing, recreational activities, and creative and educational opportunities. Prisoners were required to work, earning eighty cents a day for their labor in the camp cafeteria, in grounds maintenance, and in local construction projects. The POWs could use their wages in camp to buy toiletries, candy, cigarettes, and even beer.

"This was a far cry from the POW camps in Europe, where the Allied POWs were suffering badly. They were deprived of food and sometimes even water. Many were found malnourished when the war ended."

"I'm glad the war ended, Daddy!" Berniece exclaimed.

"So am I, darling. So am I. The war in Europe ended first, as first Italy was captured and then Germany was caught between the Americans and British coming from the west and the Russians coming from the east. Even after the European war ended, though, we still had to fight the Japanese in the Pacific. We expected that we would have to invade the Japanese islands and fight our enemies on their own soil. We expected this to be the hardest part of the entire war. A special group, including the Wildcats, was being prepared to be a 'blind' to the main Japanese army. We were to draw the attention of the Japanese army away from General MacArthur, who was planning to bring a huge army in behind the main Japanese force. They gave us our last meal. We were served a steak, English peas, and mashed potatoes. We were given a half-gunbelt of bullets because our officers didn't want the Japanese to shoot our bullets back at our armies after they took the bullets off of our dead bodies. We knew without a shadow of a doubt that we were going to die.

"What we hadn't been told was that our side had a secret weapon. American and European scientists had been busy in the United States developing a new bomb, the atomic bomb, which was more powerful than any bomb that ever had been used before. In August 1945, American planes dropped the new bomb on two Japanese cities, Hiroshima and Nagasaki. The Japanese government was stunned. They knew they could not resist us. Also, the Soviet Union had entered the war against them on the first day of August and was advancing against Japan in Korea. To save the lives of their own people, the Japanese leaders knew that they had to end the war.

"Two hours before we were scheduled to march, that march that we knew would be our last act of bravery in the war, the news was announced on the military radio that Japan had surrendered. Our group had been saved. You should have heard the shouting and cheering we raised to the skies, not only because our side had won, but because our suicide mission had been canceled. Before I left Japan, I stood guard over some of the Russian prisoners of war. They were half-starved and half-crazy from torture. We had to guard them because they would have killed every Japanese they saw. The United States troops were in charge of keeping order in Japan, but not all of us were needed. My unit was decommissioned in January 1946, and I was allowed to return home."

Berniece could hear the catch in her father's voice as he spoke. She could feel dampness on her shoulder and she knew that he had been crying as he spoke. She looked up at him. Tears were in her eyes as well.

"Daddy, you have never told me that much before. I had no idea you went through so much."

"Yes, well, honey, I don't like to remember it all the time.

But you needed to know. Now you know why Mama didn't want to hear what I was saying."

"Daddy, didn't Mama's brother, Uncle Ellis, fight some in the war, too?" Berniece asked.

"Yes, honey. He was in the navy. He was on big ships and submarines. He was also on gunboats sent out into the ocean to check out the enemy vessels and shoot on command."

"Is that what Uncle Ellis is on in that picture that Mama keeps in her dresser drawer?" Berniece asked.

"It sure is, honey," Daddy answered. "He was on the ocean for the better part of the war. He was never in Japan, but he was on many dangerous missions. We were both very lucky to get home safe and sound."

Just then Mama came around the bend of the creek. She had some sweet gum and a smile on her face.

"Just think of the two of you sitting there telling sad stories on such a beautiful day," she joked.

Berniece suspected that her mother had been hiding and listening as well, and guessed that her mother's light-hearted manner was her way of saying that she also was glad that Daddy had lived through the war and come back to Arkansas. Berniece stood, pulling her father to his feet, and embracing him in a tight hug. Then she heard her mother tease again.

"Hey, guys, are you ready to go swimming? I'll race you to the creek!"

Berniece released her father, and the three raced to the largest pool in the creek and all jumped into the water, laughing and splashing as they swam and played, enjoying each other's company—forever thankful that Daddy had come home after such a staggering ordeal.

In Asia, World War II began in July 1937 with the growth of the Japanese empire at the expense of China and other powers. The first European fighting of World War II began on September 1, 1939, when armies from Germany and the Soviet Union entered Poland, dividing the country between them. The United States did not enter World War II until December 7, 1941, when Japanese airplanes bombed Pearl Harbor in Hawaii. By the time the war ended—in May of 1945 in Europe and in August of 1945 in Japan—more than 52 million people from twenty-five nations had died, and battles had been fought in every part of the world. More than 16 million soldiers from the United States served during the war. Of that number, 291,557 died in battle, 113,842 died of other causes, and 671,846 were wounded. From Arkansas, 194,645 soldiers served in the war, of whom 3,519 were killed and roughly 2,000 more were wounded.

Nearly 16,000 people of Japanese descent—sixty-four percent of whom were American citizens—were relocated to Arkansas during the war. They stayed at camps in Rohwer and Jerome from October 1942 through December 1945. More than 23,000 German and Italian prisoners of war lived in Arkansas between 1943 and 1946. In addition to army camps and airfields, Arkansas was also home to Camp Magnolia, where 400 conscientious objectors were engaged in government projects not directly related to the war.

chapter 7

A TROUBLING PARALLEL: ARKANSAS IN THE KOREAN WAR

Jin-Ho Jenkins rode the school bus home, looking glumly out the windows at the rolling hills of Baxter County. Normally, she loved to see the beauty of the north Arkansas hills, just as she was usually excited to be starting a new year of school, and excited to have a weekend ahead of her. This September, though, everything at school seemed to be wrong. In seventh grade, she had felt popular, with friends she enjoyed and a school she liked. Now, in eighth grade, people were treating her differently, and she didn't know why. She did not see any way that she had changed.

The teasing had started the first day of school. Greg, who bullied everyone in the class, had said loudly as she came into the classroom, "Looks like we're desegregated just like down in Little Rock. We've got a dark-skinned girl in our school, too." Jin-Ho could ignore his words, but she couldn't ignore the way her other classmates laughed at his comments and stared at her with eyes that were cold and unfriendly.

The next day, Tom, who tried to make jokes about everything in school and out of school, stopped her at the door to the classroom. "You'd better watch out, Jin-Ho," he had told her. "The governor's going to send soldiers up here to keep you from coming into the school." Tom got the class to laugh, and once again people who used to be her friends looked at Jin-Ho as if she were a stranger.

Even her best friend, Julia, had put on a performance for the class. "I don't know," she said loudly at lunch that day, with mock sadness. "I just don't think, Jin-Ho, that you ever will be voted queen at the county fair." With that one sentence, Julia had both betrayed Jin-Ho's most special secret ambition, the hope she had shared only with Julia, and crushed that hope in Jin-Ho's heart.

Now, as Jin-Ho got off the bus and walked up the gravel drive to her family's house, she wished for the very first time ever that she had never come to Arkansas. For the last five years, she had liked living in Mountain Home, and she loved her family. Arkansas had always seemed a special place to her, possibly the most special place on earth. After this last week, though, Jin-Ho did not feel like her place in Mountain Home was such a great place to be after all.

As soon as she stepped into the house, her mother knew that things were not good for Jin-Ho. "What's the matter, dear?" she asked as Jin-Ho stepped into the kitchen. "Have the children at school been teasing you again?"

Jin-Ho sighed and nodded, tears welling in the corners of her eyes.

"Is it because you're adopted, honey?" her mother asked. "Don't you remember what your Daddy and I always tell you? You are extra special to us, because we got the chance to choose you and welcome you into our family."

"Oh, Mom, it's not that," Jin-Ho sobbed. She wanted to throw her schoolbooks across the kitchen, but instead she hugged them more tightly.

"Well, dear, I really want to help you figure it out, but right now I'm in the middle of making dinner. It's all of your favorite foods tonight, and I really don't want to burn anything. Maybe when your father gets home, he will be able to talk to you."

Jin-Ho ran to her room and dropped her books on the bed. Hugging her pillow, she burst into tears. Even her mother did not understand how it felt to be different from everyone else, and how it felt to have everyone else treat you as different because you *were* different.

Jin-Ho's father was Andy Jenkins. Andy worked as a mechanic in one of the garages near their hometown. He made good money. He was known as the best mechanic in Baxter County. People said that if Andy Jenkins couldn't fix a car, it wasn't worth the trouble to try to have it fixed anywhere else. Because he had a good reputation, he got a lot of work, which meant that he often

A young girl much like Jin-Ho, as photographed by U.S. soldier Jim Mullings in Seoul.
Photo courtesy of the Butler Center for Arkansas Studies.

came home late from the shop. This Friday night was no exception. Dinner was cooked and on the table, and the other members of the family were ready to sit down and eat when Andy came through the door.

"Oh, great!" he exclaimed with genuine delight when he saw the food on the table. "Fried chicken! And corn on the cob! And mashed potatoes with white gravy! And okra too!"

"And blueberry pie for dessert," his wife added, smiling. "So get your hands washed and get to this table just as fast as you can, young man!"

Nothing was said at the table about Jin-Ho's troubles at school. She wondered if the others even noticed that she was sad and quiet. Her little brother, Eric, was only four years old, so she couldn't expect him to care about her sorrows. Her parents, though, ought to be aware that something was wrong in her life. Jin-Ho was sure that they would hug her and comfort her and make things better, although she couldn't have said exactly what they would need to do to make everything right again for her.

After supper was eaten and the dishes were washed and put away, Jin-Ho walked slowly to her room. Even though he was tired, Andy responded to a silent gesture from his wife and followed Jin-Ho.

"So what's the matter, my Precious Jewel?" he asked her as they reached the doorway to her bedroom. "Why so glum this beautiful Friday night?"

Jin-Ho poured out the whole story to her father, how school was different this year, and the jokes people were making about her, and the way people looked at her differently and talked to her differently and treated her differently.

"And last year I was elected class vice-president," she went on, "but this time I wasn't nominated for any class office, not even for a spot on the student council. No one ever wants to run for student council, but even though I wanted to run, no one else would vote for me."

"Well," Andy said thoughtfully. "I'm sorry it makes you so upset. If your friends can't see how special you are, then they really are missing something important. They are the ones with the problem, though, not you. I know that doesn't make their words and actions any easier to take, but you need to believe that nothing is wrong with you—they are the ones who have a problem."

"It's so unfair, though," Jin-Ho complained. "Last year when I got an answer right in class, I felt like everyone was happy. Yesterday when I raised my hand and gave a right answer, Julia called me a show-off."

"She called you that right in front of the class?" Andy asked.

"Well, no, she whispered the word so only I could hear, but it still made me feel bad."

"I know it did," Andy said, nodding his head slowly. "I know it did."

Jin-Ho felt good that her father was willing to sit in her room and listen to her, but he didn't seem to know what to say about her problems. Eventually, he had to leave. He was tired, and he would have to get up early and get to the shop on Saturday to finish work on two cars. After he left, she sat for a while, then she pulled her world history book over to her and began idly running through the pages. Already that month they had talked about Sumeria and Egypt. Next, she knew, they would be talking about

Greece. Jin-Ho wondered if they would ever be talking about her homeland, about Korea. With a scrap of idle interest, she flipped to the index in the back of the book and looked up Korea.

The index showed that the book would talk about Korea twice: once for a page in about the middle of the book, and once more for two pages near the end of the book. Turning to the earlier reference, Jin-Ho read how Korea had once been three kingdoms that eventually combined. She read how proud the Korean people were that they had remained independent, even so close to a large country like China, and how proud they were that China negotiated with their country and treated it as an equal. Although it had been conquered once by the Mongolians, it had become independent again and remained a country of its own until Japan captured it in the year 1910.

That was interesting as history, but it did not tell Jin-Ho much about herself. With a little more curiosity, she turned to the two pages near the end of the book to see what they would say. They mentioned that, at the end of World War II, the Soviet Union had taken the north part of Korea away from Japan. Then the United States won the war and Japan surrendered. The Soviet army made a border along an imaginary line called the 38th Parallel. This line became the border between two countries with two governments, North Korea and South Korea.

Jin-Ho wondered how an imaginary line could change one country into two countries. She kept reading. She learned that, on June 25, 1950, the North Korean army had crossed the line into South Korea and almost conquered the country. But the United States had gone to the United Nations to get a group of countries together to defend South Korea. They sent their armies and fought back. Although at first they seemed to be losing, eventually they succeeded not only in driving the North Korean soldiers back across the imaginary line, but also in crossing that line themselves and invading North Korea. Then the Chinese army had arrived to help North Korea. The war went on for three years, and when it was over, the 38th Parallel was still a line between the two countries. At least two million people had died, and a lot of beautiful places had been destroyed, but other than that nothing had changed.

Finally, Jin-Ho read that the United States and North Korea and China had signed an armistice to end the war, but South Korea had never signed the armistice. Officially, the war was not over, but the bigger countries in the world made sure that the two Koreas did not cross the 38th Parallel to fight each other.

Of course Jin-Ho did not remember anything about the Japanese, who were still in control of Korea when she was born. She did remember some things about the war, but she tried hard not to think about them. She remembered the American soldiers, including Andy Jenkins, and how kind they had been to her, especially when she became an orphan. She remembered how glad she had been when he told her that the papers had been signed and he and his wife could adopt her. She remembered the long journey by plane across the Pacific Ocean to California, and the long journey by car from California to Arkansas. Most of what she remembered, though, was life in Arkansas, which had been mostly good until this month. Jin-Ho closed her eyes and cried softly until she fell asleep.

The next week was not much better for her. At school, her classmates continued to taunt her about being different, using events going on in Little Rock as ammunition for their teasing. "Do you think the president will send soldiers to Mountain Home to make sure you can go to school here?" Tom asked her one morning. Jin-Ho choked back her tears and hid her sadness as well as she could, but the way her friends and classmates treated her was still painful.

With the beauty of north Arkansas tainted for her, Jin-Ho began remembering a little more of her old home back in Korea. She had lived in a hilly region on the west end of the country, not far south from the 38th Parallel. When the North Koreans first had attacked, they must have ignored her town in their drive to capture Seoul, the capital of South Korea. Then the United States and the other countries sent by the United Nations had pushed the North Koreans away again. Most of the men from her village had left to fight in the South Korean army, but her mother and her neighbors had believed that they were safe, that the war was happening somewhere else and would not come to bother them.

One day, disaster struck. Jin-Ho was out looking for bird eggs to take to her mother. She was climbing up the face of a steep cliff. Suddenly, she heard a loud blast close to her village. The cliff she was on shook, but luckily she could climb into a small cave on the face of the cliff before she was shaken off or smashed by a falling rock. Jin-Ho was terrified. She didn't know what had happened, but she knew that it was something terrible. She hid in the cave all night. Finally, near noon the next day, hunger drove her out. She needed to find out what had happened to her home, her mother, her two sisters, and her younger brother.

Jin-Ho was weak from hunger when she stumbled into her village. To her horror, she saw what was once her village was a smoking pile of rubble. It was obvious that the North Koreans and Chinese had been there. As Jin-Ho stumbled through the village, she realized that her mother and siblings were all dead, along with her uncles, aunts, and cousins—her entire family. She leaned against an old tree that had been in her village for years and cried uncontrollably. Her body would not stop shaking. She felt herself sink to the ground. The next thing she knew, Andy Jenkins had her in his arms. He said, "Come on, honey, everything is going to be all right. I'll keep you with me."

This was not the first time Jin-Ho had met Andy Jenkins. He had been in Company B, Sixth Infantry Regiment, Second Infantry Division of the U.S. Army. He was stationed near Tongmong in Korea. His company lived in a group of tents that were arranged like a small village. They had taught the children a few simple English phrases, like "thank you" and "see you later." Jin-Ho, as well as the other children of her village, would often visit the soldiers. Sometimes, she would bring fresh eggs or vegetables to the soldiers to exchange for a chocolate bar.

Jin-Ho especially liked Andy Jenkins. He was always friendly and often told her of his home state, Arkansas. He described the beautiful terrain, such as the creek and cliffs around his home near Mountain Home. He often talked about fishing around the Bull Shoals Dam or floating the Buffalo River when he was a child. He loved his country so much that Jin-Ho could almost see the beauty as she listened to him talk, even if she couldn't understand most of the words he said.

Andy kept his word and had taken care of Jin-Ho. He managed to adopt her and bring her back to his homeland near Mountain Home. Andy's wife, Carrie, welcomed her with open arms. Jin-Ho's life was drastically changed. She had been in Arkansas for five years. She could hardly remember her village in Korea. Only her recent sense of loss had brought memories of her first home back into her mind again.

Friday morning came again, and, to her surprise, Andy met Jin-Ho before she left the house to wait for the school bus.

"Wait just a minute, Precious Jewel," her father said to her. "I want to show you something from the newspaper."

The paper he showed her was not a local newspaper. Those came out once a week and contained only stories about Mountain Home and the other small towns near it and the people who lived in Baxter County. Andy was holding a newspaper from Little Rock. On the front page was a photograph of a large high school, with a crowd of people gathered in front of it.

"Do you see this, honey?" her father asked her, in a voice she had not heard before, a voice that was gentle, yet urgent. "Do you see those nine brave children, walking in the front doors of that high school, even though all those other people want them to go away? Think how brave they are, Precious Jewel. Think how hard it is for them to go to that school, and think of all the mean and cruel things people are saying to them."

He added, "I know people have said some of the same things to you recently. I am proud of you, Jin-Ho. You don't have to be as brave as those nine children in Little Rock, but you are still as brave as you need to be. Today, I hope you will stand up straight and hold your head up high. Be proud of who you are, my Precious Jewel. You are very special, and anyone who cannot see that is just not paying attention."

Andy had not told her to do anything different from what she had been doing all month, and yet the fact that he had said those words made a difference to Jin-Ho. After all, he knew what it was to be brave. He had been a soldier for his country, which had sent him to fight for people like her in her country. He had cared enough to bring her home with him to Arkansas and make her part of his family.

More than that, Jin-Ho remembered that she *was* different after all. She came from a proud people who had a long history of independence and strength. She found that she could stand up straight and hold her head up high. When Greg and Tom and the others teased her, it did not seem so bad. After all, they had already used up their jokes, and they did not sound so funny the second and third time. Even when Julia and the other girls snubbed her, it did not hurt as much as before. Jin-Ho discovered, as she rode the bus home that afternoon, that she was no longer as sad or as angry as she had been a week before.

When Jin-Ho got off the bus, her younger brother came running to meet her. He was four years old with beautiful blond curls cascading all over his head. His mother and his father were also her mother and father, even if she had first been born into another family on the other side of the world. Jin-Ho picked Eric up and whirled him around in the air before putting him down again. They ran into the house laughing.

North and South Korea were created when the land of Korea was divided at the 38th Parallel in 1945. On June 25, 1950, North Korea invaded South Korea. The United States and other members of the United Nations sent troops to defend South Korea. Soldiers from China entered the conflict to fight on behalf of North Korea. In the end, the conflict involved fighters from twenty-two nations. As many as four million people died or were badly injured, including one million civilians in South Korea and one million civilians in North Korea, as well as 900,000 Chinese soldiers, 520,000 North Korean soldiers, and 313,000 South Korean soldiers. By the time of the armistice, signed on July 27, 1953, the United States had involved 5,720,000 service members in the conflict. A total of 36,574 American soldiers died in action, and another 17,672 died in service but not in battle; more than 100,000 more American soldiers were injured in the conflict. From Arkansas, 6,300 men and women served in the conflict, of whom 461 died.

In September 1957, nine African American students sought to attend classes at segregated Central High School in Little Rock. Governor Faubus sent the Arkansas National Guard to the school grounds to prevent rioting and, following his orders, the soldiers barred the nine students from the school. Later that month, President Eisenhower sent the United States Army's 101st Airborne Division to Little Rock to guarantee the safety of the nine students at the high school while they attended classes. The desegregation of Central High School in Little Rock captured the attention of people, not only throughout Arkansas, but across the nation and in much of the world.

MORE THAN A DIFFERENCE OF OPINION: THE VIETNAM WAR

On a sunny afternoon in the summer of 1977, the sounds of war echoed in the air of an otherwise quiet neighborhood in Mena, Arkansas. Charlie Trammell and his best friend, Gary Lane, were pretending to be American soldiers helping to capture France back from the Nazis in June of 1944. Their friends Bobby and Mark Parsons fought for the Germans. Sticks and broom handles sufficed as rifles, the boys' voices provided most of the sound effects, and imagination took care of the rest. The entire neighborhood was a battlefield, and the Germans had to be outwitted and captured before suppertime was announced by any of their mothers.

Charlie and Gary and Mark were all twelve. Bobby, the youngest of a family of nine children, was two years younger than the others. The boys had grown up together in Mena, played together in the yards and streets of their neighborhood every weekend and every summer except when it rained, and often ate meals and even spent the night at each other's houses. Usually, they were the best of friends, except for those times when a passing argument or the rules of a game required them to be fierce opponents.

Gary offered his planned strategy to Charlie. "You go around the right side of the house, I'll go around the left, we'll catch them between us and capture them and win the war."

"No," Charlie objected. "It won't work. They'll be expecting us. They were expecting us the last time we tried that, and the time before..."

"Well, at least it's an idea. Do you have a better idea?"

Charlie had wanted to suggest his idea for several days. "You go to the corner of the house and draw them out to the street. I'll

hide on the porch of the 'haunted house,' and when they come past
me, I'll stand up and shoot them both before they get to you."

"Boo's house?!" Gary was impressed. For as long as the boys
could remember—three or four years, at least—the Franklin house
had been the "haunted house" to all of them. They would not go
near it after dark and hardly dared to look at it even in the daylight.
Only since spring, when he had read *To Kill a Mockingbird* in
school, had Gary begun calling it "Boo's house." He acted as if he
knew a secret and wanted the others to ask, which is why Charlie
never asked him why he called it Boo's house.

"It will be a big surprise. It should work. But are you sure
you're brave enough to hide on Boo's porch?" Gary challenged
him. If Charlie had held any doubts about his plan before the
challenge, they disappeared now. A grim and serious soldier on a
deadly but necessary mission, he grabbed his rifle, nodded once,
and crept toward the porch.

The young soldiers had not discussed exactly how Gary was
going to draw the enemy troop out toward the street. As Charlie
slipped silently into position, he wondered what Gary would
improvise for that part of the plan. He noted his surroundings:
the porch had not been swept or cleaned in ages. It was covered
with dust and dirt, spider webs, and even leaves left from last
November or so. Charlie took his position in the back corner
of the porch, where he could peer over the edge. If the enemy
expected an attack from that quarter, he knew they would see
his head, but he was confident they would not expect him to
be there. Intent on watching for his partner and for the pursuit,
Charlie did not notice the open window—or see the arm reaching
out, the hand ready to grasp his shoulder.

Of course the firm, manly grip took him completely by
surprise. To his credit, he did not struggle to run away or even
cry out in terror. Instead, he turned to look, half expecting that
Gary was playing a trick on him. Instead, he saw an unfamiliar
face in the window: piercing blue eyes, dark blond hair longer
than Charlie was accustomed to seeing on a man, short blond
beard, and chiseled nose. Trembling, but still determined to keep
control of himself, Charlie could only ask the one-word question, "Boo?"

"Don't call me that!" the man snapped back in anger. He continued to hold Charlie's shoulder, but spoke with slightly less anger as he said, "If you're going to make fun of me, you might as well at least know my name. I am Private Daniel Franklin, 9th Infantry Division, APC. My serial number is RA11860007."

"We weren't making fun of you," Charlie protested. "We were only playing army-man."

"Well, now you get to meet a real army-man, son. Come inside the house, and I'll tell you a real war story."

Charlie felt torn. He was more than a little scared of Daniel, and he wasn't sure if he should go into Daniel's house without checking first with his mother. On the other hand, he had been told always to be polite to strangers, and he was interested enough to hear Daniel's stories.

"Can't you come out here?" he asked cautiously.

Daniel thought for a minute. "All right," he said, releasing Charlie's shoulder. "I'll come out there. Anything to stop you boys from playing war games in my front yard."

Half a minute later, the front door opened. Daniel stepped out onto the porch. His skin was pale, as if he had not seen the sun for more than a year. He hobbled out on crutches, although he did not have a cast on either leg. In fact, his legs looked smaller than normal, as if they had been damaged some time in the past. Daniel moved across the porch and sat down on the brick ledge that served as a half-wall and had been Charlie's hiding place. Seeing that Charlie was looking at his legs, he grunted, "VA is supposed to get me a wheelchair and a ramp to get in and out of the house, but so far they haven't gotten around to it. That's why you never see me outside."

"Are you a disabled vet?" asked Charlie. He had heard the phrase before but had never thought about what it meant.

"That's right, son. I was injured fighting for your country in Vietnam, back when you were just a little boy. Other wars had heroes, but I guess I'm just a disabled vet."

"I'm sorry. I didn't mean to hurt your feelings. I don't know what I should say, but I do want to hear the story you promised to tell." Charlie could see Gary and Mark and Bobby watching from his back yard. Suddenly he felt proud of himself, meeting Daniel and talking to him on his front porch after they had been afraid of his house all those years. Charlie looked forward to boasting to his friends later and repeating all the exciting things that he was about to learn.

"OK, son, here's my story: It was early on the morning of January 30th. We were stationed just outside of Saigon. I was with the armored personnel carriers, or APCs, which meant driving and using tanks. We were surprise-attacked by the Viet Cong. They called this the Tet Offensive. It was named after the Vietnamese holiday they were celebrating at that time. The Viet Cong struck many urban places at the same time. Back at the end of 1967, the United States had 485,000 troops all over Vietnam. All of them were hit pretty hard. Our tunnel rats were climbing in and out of the tunnels like crazy trying to get the advantage of the Viet Cong. The fighting continued off and on for three long weeks.

"The 9th Infantry, which was an Army unit, was stationed near Saigon. A troop raced for Bien Hoa with only one tank. When we entered the city of Bien Hoa, which was between Saigon and the air base, we found the town square full of people. Because we knew we had to reach the air base quickly, we just kept moving through the crowd. Soon, we realized that we were in the middle of the Viet Cong and NOA soldiers. The Viet Cong quickly recovered from their surprise at seeing us. They burst into our midst and opened fire on the passing vehicles. The second platoon, alerted by the firing, drove into the square with all its machine guns blazing. We were able to pick up the disabled crews and continue on. The troop only had one tank and eight ACAVs, which were Army Cavalry Assault Vehicles, at this point.

"The squadron commander joined the troops from his helicopter and directed them through the narrow maze of city streets and out again toward the air base by the quickest route. We soon spotted several Viet Cong in the ditches on both sides of the road where they were waiting for an attack. We spotted them, so we swung off the road and drove parallel to it. As the Viet Cong passed, we ambushed from the rear, inflicting heavy damage on the enemy. They suffered heavy casualties. Our commander, who was still circling above us, was almost blown out of the air by the force of the ground explosion of the bunker of ammunition at

Long Bink. We were fortunate that any of us survived. We continued to fight on the ground, sometimes in hand-to-hand combat.

"I have to say, my battalion was hit hard. Wounded men lay everywhere. My friends went down one by one in front of my eyes. I could do nothing. I had made expert marksman in all weaponry, and all I could do was just shoot back at the Viet Cong as my comrades lay dying. I was involved with the most brutal battle. Near the end, we were doing some hand-to-hand combat until the air support came in. Suddenly, I felt a sharp pain in my back. I knew I'd been hit.

"The next thing I knew, I woke up in a Saigon hospital. I was later told that, by the time darkness fell and the situation began to stabilize, the tank had been hit nineteen times, and the crew had been replaced twice. They tell me that I was out for three or four days. This was considered one of the worst ground attacks of the war. The Viet Cong lost many soldiers also. In fact, they didn't launch another major offensive for years because of all their losses in that one attack."

"Are you sorry you fought in the war?" Charlie asked quietly.

"Sorry?" Daniel asked, and then he cursed. "No, I'm not sorry. I went to Vietnam so people like you would remain free. I didn't want communism to spread. I wanted to be sure that democracy would still exist when you are an adult. People called me names when I came back from the war. They said I was a baby-killer and an enemy of humanity, but I didn't care. I never cared what people said about me, as long as I knew I was fighting to keep my country free."

"Thank you very much," Charlie said, not sure whether to call his neighbor Daniel or Mr. Franklin or maybe Private Franklin. Instead he said, "My friends are waiting for me. I'm glad you told me your story. I hope we can visit again some time."

"Take care, Charlie," Daniel said, pulling himself upright on his crutches and hobbling back across the porch to the front door.

Just as Charlie reached his friends in the back yard, his mother called that supper was ready.

"Mom," he yelled back, "can Gary and Bobby and Mark stay for supper?"

"As long as their parents say it's OK," Mrs. Trammel answered. "We're having spaghetti." The boys raced to their homes, made their persuasive arguments to their parents, and were soon back at the Trammel residence, eager for spaghetti but far more eager to hear Charlie's story.

Charlie's mother listened intently as he repeated as much as he could remember of Daniel's account. When he finished, she said quietly, "Danny was always an active boy, just like the four of you. As soon as he turned eighteen and finished high school, he signed up to serve in the army; he didn't even wait to find out whether or not he would be drafted. I was sad to hear he had been injured, and I'm sad to think of him sitting in that house day after day for all these years. His mother lives there, too, and she goes out and buys groceries and things, but neither of them ever talks to anyone. I'm glad Danny finally spoke to you."

After a pause, she added, "This could be good for Danny and good for all of you as well. Why don't you see if he will eat lunch with you tomorrow? I'll give you money for take-out pizza from the new place down the street. Let me call the Franklins and see if Danny will visit with you tomorrow noon over pizza."

"Aw, Mom," Charlie began, but she gave him the look that always meant that no argument would be allowed. True to her word, she did call the Franklin house and talk with Mrs. Franklin and arrange the lunch date. True to her word, she gave Charlie seven dollars the next morning before she left for work, reminding him to pick up two large pepperoni pizzas at twelve o'clock and bring them to the Franklin house as she had promised.

Charlie felt a bit silly carrying the two pizza boxes a block and a half from the restaurant to the Franklin house. He also felt strange walking boldly up the stairs of a house he had feared and avoided for so long. Gary and Mark had waited for him on the sidewalk in front of the house. "Where's Bobby?" Charlie asked.

"Bobby's scared. He's being a baby," Mark answered. Charlie did not point out that Mark looked scared as well, and so did Gary, since Charlie was beginning to feel a little scared himself. It was one thing to speak with Daniel on the porch; it was another to be invited into the "haunted house", even with two of his friends and two pizzas.

Daniel must have seen Charlie coming up the street, because he opened the door while Charlie was still trying to figure out how to knock with both hands full.

"Come in," he invited, and in an apologizing tone he added, "Mom set this up for me and told me to let you in and eat with you and answer your questions, but she's staying upstairs while you are here. Mom's not real good with company."

The living room had an old television set in one corner, and a couch and two chairs that looked like they were twenty years old and had been falling apart for the last ten years. A low table in the middle of the room seemed the right place to set the pizza boxes, so Charlie did just that. Daniel dropped himself into a chair, and the boys sat on the floor. Charlie opened the boxes, and they began to eat.

They each ate a piece or two in silence before Daniel finally spoke.

"So, were you supposed to ask me questions, or what?" he challenged the boys.

U.S. soldier Fred Campbell and South Vietnamese Infantry Interpreter Trung Kim Qui pose in Vietnam; Private Daniel Franklin probably enjoyed similar light-hearted moments during his service in the Vietnam War. Photo courtesy of the Museum of American History, Cabot Public Schools.

"Could you start," Charlie replied timidly, "by telling them what you told me last night, about the tanks and Tet and all that?"

Daniel's mouth smiled, although his eyes shone with an edge of anger or perhaps fear of the memory. The account he gave was nearly word-for-word the way he had spoken it to Charlie the night before, as if he had practiced this speech a few times over the years. When he finished, the boys looked up at him, for a moment at a loss of what to say.

Gary was the first to break the silence. "Nothing against you, but it's too bad you had to go all that way to fight a war that wasn't necessary. My dad says that the Vietnam War was the biggest waste of lives and of money in our country's history."

Daniel did not hesitate to answer. "Our country fought that war so people could be free over there and people could stay free here as well. What would your father have wanted our government to do, wait until the communists had conquered every other country in the world and we were the only free country left?"

"But the communists *did* win in Vietnam. For the first time in history, America lost a war, and we lost because it was a war we never should have fought."

"No," Daniel disagreed, "we won the war, but we lost the peace. A cease-fire was signed in January 1973 that ended the war and brought all our soldiers home, even the prisoners of war, and North Vietnam promised not to invade South Vietnam. Two years later, they broke the treaty and the United States did nothing to stop them. We had beaten them on the battlefield time and time again, which is why they negotiated with us to end the war."

"My father says that we could have had the same treaty years earlier, but we were too stubborn to end the war until then," Mark said.

"That's not true either," Daniel said. "I've read about the negotiations in Paris, and the North Vietnamese were asking impossible things until they realized in 1972 that we couldn't be beaten. They are the ones who conceded and made an armistice possible. South Vietnam didn't want to sign the armistice, because they were afraid it would be broken and we would do nothing about it. As it turned out, they were right. We did win the war, but we lost the peace."

"We still never should have fought that war," Gary insisted.

"My sister was a student up in Fayetteville during the war," Mark added. "She marched in protests and demanded that we get out of the war. My father was very proud of her. He says that she is the one who was standing up for her country."

"Your sister probably made the war longer instead of shorter," Daniel countered. "She gave the enemy hope that the United States would give up and leave. As the president said—and I remember this speech he gave—no other country can defeat the United States. Only Americans can weaken us."

"That's the same president who made the war bigger, sending soldiers into Cambodia and Laos," Gary reminded Daniel. "He said that he wanted 'peace with honor,' but he made the war bigger and made it last longer."

"He only sent soldiers where the enemy was," Daniel said, raising his voice. "The Cambodian government never complained when we attacked the enemy that was hiding in their country. The president did what he had to do to defeat the enemy and bring us soldiers home. As it is now, communists are taking over in Cambodia and Laos, too, and more people are dying because we didn't maintain the peace by forcing them to honor the treaty."

Mark stood up and said, "Americans think we always have to be fighting communists, but maybe the people over there wanted to be communists. Did you ever think of that?"

Daniel had an answer ready. "When Vietnam was first divided, the north half communist and the south half free, one million people fled from the north to the south. How many fled from the south to the north? In 1975, thousands of people did whatever they could to escape the communists. They clung to helicopters taking off; they escaped in boats so full they began to sink. Americans helped rescue the people from Vietnam who didn't want to be communist. Those people risked their lives to come live here today; some of them even came to Arkansas. The way they ran away from their own land tells me everything I need to know about why we fought that war."

Gary and Mark both began to shout responses, but Charlie

interrupted them both. "We don't need to start another war here," he told them when they were quiet. "This argument could go on all afternoon, and not one of you is going to change his mind. Mr. Franklin, thank you for letting us share lunch with you, and thank you for answering our questions."

"Charlie, thank you for the pizza," Daniel said. "Boys, you are free to play on my lawn any time. You can even come up on the porch. And, Charlie, once in a while I hope you'll knock on the door so we can visit some more."

Indochina was a French colony until Japan captured it during World War II. After the war ended, several groups sought to govern parts of Indochina, and the French eventually divided the area into Cambodia, Laos, and Vietnam. In 1954, Vietnam was divided into two countries, one allied with the Soviet Union and the other with the United States, much as Korea and Germany had been divided earlier. The United States sent military advisors to help the South Vietnamese government resist the Viet Cong, who had entered the country to fight for communism in the south at the same time that a million refugees were fleeing North Vietnam. American involvement in the war grew, and between 1964 and 1972, 3,403,000 American troops were deployed to Vietnam. More than 500,000 Americans were fighting in the war in early 1969, after which time the size of the American force in combat was gradually reduced. A treaty was signed in January 1973 that promised peace in Vietnam and ended American military involvement there. In December 1974, North Vietnam again attacked South Vietnam, which proved unable to defend itself. By the end of April 1975, Vietnam had been united under the North Vietnamese government.

During the war, from 1954 through 1975, five million Vietnamese died, four million of them civilians. A total 90,209 American soldiers died in the conflict and 153,303 more were wounded. A total of 622 soldiers from Arkansas died or were missing in the conflict. American involvement in the war was controversial at the time and remains controversial today. Never since the American Revolution had the United States been involved in any war for more than four years. Improved communications, especially television, made the realities of war more apparent to Americans than they had been for a century. After the war ended, 50,809 Vietnamese refugees were housed at Fort Chaffee, near Fort Smith, Arkansas, until homes in the United States could be found for them. Many of those Vietnamese families eventually made their homes in Arkansas.

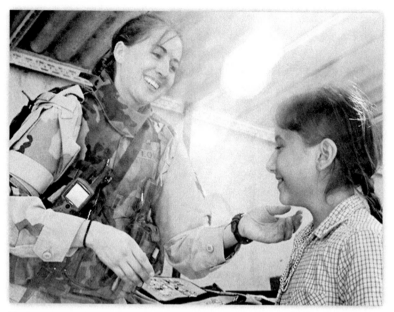

First Lieutenant Robin Lowery visiting an orphanage in Iraq in 2004 on a mission similar to that of Dr. Jessica Branson. Photo courtesy of the Arkansas National Guard State Public Affairs Office, taken by Capt. Chris Heathscott.

chapter 9

CHANGING LIVES AND THROWING STONES: WARS IN AFGHANISTAN AND IRAQ

The all-school assembly at Washington Junior High School in Bentonville was dismissed, and students were sent to their homerooms before the end of the day. It was Monday, September 11, 2006, five years after terrorist attacks had destroyed the World Trade Center buildings in New York City and damaged the Pentagon in Washington DC. Teachers and other adults talked about the attacks as fresh memories that were still shocking and painful. Curt Cooper, like his classmates, had been only seven years old the day of the attacks. He remembered seeing television pictures of the airplanes hitting the towers and of the towers falling to the ground, but now that he was twelve those same pictures seemed less dramatic than many other scenes he had witnessed on news programs or in movies.

Coming into the classroom, Curt and his classmates were not talking about the assembly or the events it remembered. Instead, Travis Morgan was sharing news he had picked up over the weekend.

"I hear that some Arabs are moving into that empty house down the street from you," Travis commented to Curt.

"That's just what our school needs," sneered Wyatt Jones. "We've got Mexican kids and black kids and Vietnamese kids and Cherokee kids. Now we'll have Arab terrorists in the school, too. Better watch out, Curt, or they'll be trying to blow up your house."

Mr. Owens, their homeroom teacher, usually did not pay much attention to conversations between the students, but this time was different.

"What's this about Arab terrorists in the school?" he asked the boys.

"Didn't you hear?" Travis replied. "An Arab family bought the house on G Street."

"The Akbar family is not from Arabia," Mr. Owens commented. "They come from Pakistan."

"How do you know where they come from?" asked Travis.

Mr. Owens smiled. "Shiraz Akbar will be starting school here by the end of the week. In fact, she will be part of this homeroom. That's why I know a little bit about them."

"But Pakistan is one of the Arab countries, anyhow, isn't it?" Wyatt asked.

"Not at all!" exclaimed Mr. Owens. To the surprise of the students, he pulled a wall map down from its roller. Mr. Owens was a math teacher, and it never occurred to his homeroom students that he would take an interest in geography.

"Now, look," he continued, pointing to the map. "This map shows southwest Asia, which a lot of Americans call the Middle East. This large section of land is Arabia. That's where Arabs come from. Egypt is on this side of Arabia, in the corner of Africa, and Israel is north of Arabia, on the Mediterranean Sea, and farther north is Turkey, where Asia and Europe meet. Over here is Iraq, including the Tigris and Euphrates rivers, where civilization began, and past Iraq is Iran, and beyond Iran is Afghanistan, and finally we get to Pakistan, next to India. In fact, for most of history, Pakistan was part of India. The people of Pakistan are different in many ways from the people of Arabia."

"Aren't they all Muslim terrorists? That's what I thought the news people said on TV last night," Karen commented.

"The people in Pakistan, and Iraq and Iran and Afghanistan, and Turkey and Egypt and Arabia—most of them are Muslims. Not all Muslims are terrorists, though. In fact, a great many Muslims are opposed to terrorist groups, just like people everywhere. Calling all Muslims Arabs, or calling all Muslims terrorists, shows that you really don't understand what's going on in the world."

"Why are we fighting a war against them if they aren't terrorists?" Maria demanded.

The bell rang as Mr. Owens began his answer, but the students stayed in their seats, wanting to hear what he would say.

"I don't have time to answer that question today," he admitted, "but I think tomorrow we will take a break from math, and I will try to explain the wars we are fighting and have fought recently. In fact, I am going to arrange to have three soldiers talk to you tomorrow. Maybe they will be able to answer your questions."

Curt and the other students grabbed their books and backpacks and headed for the door. On his way home from school, Curt passed the house that had just been bought. A large truck was in the road, and three men were unloading boxes and furniture. Curt did not see anyone at the house who looked foreign, but then he did not suppose he would know how a person from Pakistan should look.

He mentioned the new family to his father while the two of them ate dinner that night. Martha Cooper, Curt's mother, was working the evening shift at the hospital, so Ken Cooper, Curt's father, had picked up some Chinese food on his way home from the office. Curt doused his second eggroll in sweet-and-sour sauce and then remarked, "Travis says that the new family down the street are Arab terrorists, but Mr. Owens said they are from Pakistan. He showed us a map with the countries on it, but I still don't understand what he was trying to say."

"We have a book with maps in it," his father answered. "Maybe we should look at it together after supper."

The book was a historical atlas, showing major civilizations and empires throughout the history of the world. Curt was surprised to see how many of those major civilizations were based in southwest Asia. He had heard of Egypt and the pyramids before, but he was amazed to discover that some cities in southern Iraq were even older. His father pointed out to him the various empires that had begun in Iraq: the Akkadians, the Assyrians, the Babylonians, and the Abbasids. They also found maps that showed how the area had been part of other empires: the Persians from Iran, Mongols from eastern Asia, Ottomans from Turkey, and, after them, the British.

"Is it true that people in that part of the world are always fighting?" Curt asked his father.

"People have lived there for a long time," his father answered, "and we are talking about a fairly large part of the world. I guess people there are like people everywhere: sometimes they get along, and sometimes they fight. It's hard to find any part of the world where people have managed to stay out of fights for much of their history."

The next morning, Curt and his classmates expected to see three soldiers in uniform in their classroom. Mr. Owens had promised that they would hear from three soldiers, but the only adults in the classroom when school began were Mr. Owens and Dr. Branson, Cheyenne's mother. Curt remembered that Cheyenne had spoken about her mother being in the National Guard, but he always thought of her as a doctor, not a soldier.

The bell rang, and Mr. Owens stood up and began speaking. "I promised yesterday that you would hear from three soldiers this morning. I didn't tell you that I am one of those soldiers." The students gasped; they thought of Mr. Owens as a math teacher, and most of them could not picture him as a soldier. "When I graduated from high school twenty years ago, I joined the U.S. Air Force. After a couple of transfers, I ended up at the Little Rock Air Force Base in Jacksonville. That's where I was stationed when Iraq invaded Kuwait, beginning the first Gulf War."

"Were you a fighter pilot? Did you drop bombs on Iraq?" the students asked.

Mr. Owens laughed. "Not exactly. I worked on large transport planes called C-130s, and I didn't fly them. My group was responsible for getting the planes loaded or unloaded. That fall and winter, we were busy here in Arkansas loading planes to bring troops and equipment over to Saudi Arabia. Then, when the war was over, my group was flown to Saudi Arabia to load the planes there so we could bring our soldiers and equipment back home."

"So you never actually fought in the war," Sean said.

"A lot of men and women in uniform don't actually fight. A lot more is involved in war than just firing guns or dropping bombs. Getting our soldiers there with supplies and equipment and getting them back home again was a big and important job. In Saudi Arabia, I worked with some fine men and women from Illinois and Indiana whose job was to pack and store all the things that we flew home from there. They were as important to the war effort as anyone who fired a gun or who dropped a bomb."

Curt raised his hand. "Tell us why we were fighting over there in the first place," he asked.

Travis added, before Mr. Owens could reply, "My mother says we have no business fighting wars in the Middle East. She says the United States should stop trying to be police for the entire world."

"I've been thinking most of the night how to explain the Gulf War," Mr. Owens admitted. "It's hard to know where to start; the beginnings of the fighting seem to go earlier and earlier the more I think about them. Probably I should begin at the end of the 1970s, when both Iran and Iraq had important changes in their governments. Before that time, the United States had been working with both countries, largely because we didn't want the Soviet Union to gain too much influence in that part of the world. The change of government in Iran was violent. The Shah of Iran was overthrown and a man named Khomeini set up a new government, which he said was based on the rules of their religion, Islam. Both Americans and Soviets were considered enemies of Iran, and several dozen Americans were captured and held hostage in Iran for more than a year. Meanwhile, a man named Saddam Hussein was gradually gaining control of the government in Iraq. By the end of 1979, both Khomeini and Saddam Hussein were in control of their countries, and the next year Iran and Iraq declared war on each other.

"The United States wasn't directly involved in that war, which lasted for eight years, but I mention it this morning because of what followed. In 1990, Iraq was trying to escape the debt it owed because of money it had borrowed to fight that war. On August 2, the Iraqi army entered Kuwait, a small country just south of Iraq on the Persian Gulf. Saddam Hussein claimed that Kuwait should have been part of Iraq all along. A lot of other issues were involved as well. The United States government spoke against the invasion, and the United Nations voted to condemn it. In November, the United Nations set a deadline of January 15 for Iraq to get its army out of Kuwait, but American troops had already been sent to Saudi Arabia as early as the 7th of the previous August. In the end, thirty-four nations cooperated in the effort to set Kuwait free from Iraq.

"After the deadline passed in January, Iraq was attacked on bombing missions and with missiles. They fought back with missiles aimed at our camps in Saudi Arabia and also aimed at Israel. Most of their Scud missiles were ineffective, because our American forces had developed Patriot missiles that were usually successful at meeting and destroying their missiles before they reached their target. Saddam's attempt to provoke a reaction from Israel that might have split apart the coalition also failed. On February 24, the land invasion began. By February 28, Iraqi troops were fleeing Kuwait, and a cease-fire was declared."

"Why didn't the United States finish the job then and overthrow Saddam Hussein?" Sean asked.

"We didn't overthrow Saddam in 1991 because we hadn't said that was our goal. The thirty-four–nation coalition was working together only to free Kuwait. When the Iraqi soldiers left Kuwait, we had accomplished the one thing we said we wanted to do."

He added, "Remember, though, that through the 1990s, the United States kept watch over Iraq. Several times, our military forces acted to keep the army of Iraq from doing things we had prohibited, either against its own citizens or as a threat to its neighbors. The second Gulf War, which began in 2003, was designed to overthrow Saddam, but we have another conflict to discuss before we get to that. I think it is time for me to introduce our guest, Doctor Jessica Branson, who has served two terms in Afghanistan for our armed forces."

"Thank you, Mr. Owens," Dr. Branson said. "I wonder how many of you students would be able to find Afghanistan on a map?" Most members of the class, including Curt, raised their hands. "That is good," she said. "When I was your age, I didn't even know that there was a country called Afghanistan. That part of the world didn't seem to have anything to do with my life. I knew about Germany and Japan, but I didn't know anything about places like Afghanistan.

"The people of that country have faced a lot of changes over the last hundred years. The British fought to control that part of the world until World War I ended. Then it became a kingdom until 1973, when the government was changed again and it became a republic. Several different groups of people tried to take control of the country, and, in 1979, the Soviet Union sent forces to help one of those groups. The United States didn't send fighters into Afghanistan during that time, but we did train and equip some of the groups who were fighting against the Soviets. After ten years, the Soviet Union finally withdrew its troops from Afghanistan, and after several more years of fighting, a group that called itself the Taliban emerged as the government."

Maria raised her hand and asked, "Isn't the Taliban a terrorist group that hates women?"

"The Taliban, like Khomeini's government in Iran, believed that a certain form of the Muslim religion, Islam, should determine all the laws of the country. Even most Muslims in other parts of the world disagreed with many of the Taliban's rules. They didn't allow women to hold certain professional jobs or even to be educated outside the home. They destroyed artwork from other religions. The Taliban also supported various groups of terrorists who were trying to bring the same kind of thinking to other parts of the world. One of those groups was led by an Arab man named Osama bin Laden."

This was a name the students all recognized; it had been mentioned more than once in the Patriot Day assembly.

"The United States had helped to train and equip his group in the 1980s, since he was one of those fighting against the Soviet presence in Afghanistan. After the first Gulf War, bin Laden expressed his anger that American soldiers and others who were not Muslims had camped in Saudi Arabia during the war and remained in the country after the war, and the group he formed (called al-Qaeda) began attacking American military installations and other property in various parts of the world. On August 7, 1998, al-Qaeda attacked and blew up American embassies in Kenya and Tanzania. In response, our president ordered missile strikes against al-Qaeda camps in Sudan and in Afghanistan. Al-Qaeda has performed many other terrorist acts, but the most famous of them was of course the attacks on the World Trade Center and the Pentagon five years ago."

Travis did not raise his hand. He asked, "Why did we go to

war in Afghanistan if bin Laden and al-Qaeda were the people
who attacked us? They were not the Taliban; those are two different groups."

"Our government knew that bin Laden and the other leaders
of al-Qaeda were in Afghanistan. They offered the Taliban a
chance to turn over the terrorist leaders for justice, but the
Taliban refused. As a result, on October 7, 2001, American forces
attacked Afghanistan. By the end of the year, the major cities of
the country were under our control, although several al-Qaeda
leaders and Taliban leaders escaped capture and are still at large
today. Since that time, American forces and soldiers from other
countries have been trying to battle terrorists and keep the peace
in Afghanistan while supporting the new government in its
efforts to build a better life for its people."

Dr. Branson smiled at the students. "I have served two six-
month tours of duty in Afghanistan. Sometimes it saddens me to
see the people who have been hurt by the war, and people who are
still being hurt as terrorists try to destroy the new Afghanistan
we are helping to strengthen. Not all my work is with war-related
injuries, though. I give children shots to keep them from getting
sick. I teach parents about good health practices for themselves
and their families. Of course, I see to the needs of our own troops
stationed over there. A large part of my job is to make a good
impression on the people of Afghanistan so they won't be afraid
of Americans. They have been told that our ways are bad and that
all of us are evil; just by being in their country and being friendly
and helpful, I have helped to show the people there that we are
not so bad.

"I've seen some terribly sad things in Afghanistan. I've seen
Afghan men come into our camps to be trained, only to turn
around and sell their boots and equipment to buy food for their
children. I've seen people come to our camps, begging just for
permission to eat the scraps of food we put into the garbage. I've
heard of women who were stoned to death by people in their
villages merely because they wanted to have the rights that we
take for granted in this country. But when I am in Afghanistan, I
also see hope. People who have known nothing but poverty and
war all their lives are learning that life doesn't have to be that

way. I am proud to be serving my country, not fighting a war with guns and bombs, but bringing new ideas and hope to people in another part of the world."

The students sat quietly listening as Dr. Branson spoke. When she was done, several raised their hands to ask questions, but Mr. Owens interrupted them.

"There will be time for more questions in a little bit," he said, looking at his watch, "but we need to hear first from our third soldier. He isn't here in this room; he is in Iraq right now. Sean's older brother Willy is a former student at this school, and he agreed to talk with us over the Internet." Glancing at his watch again, Mr. Owens added, "It is nearly nine o'clock here, which means that it is six in the evening there. Sergeant Stotts has agreed to begin visiting with us at exactly six o'clock his time. Let me see if I can get him on the computer."

"Your brother is doing a podcast?" Karen asked Sean.

"No, not a podcast," Mr. Owens explained. "A podcast is like a TV show or radio show sent on the Internet. This is going to be a two-way conversation. Willy will be able to listen to us as well as speak with us." Mr. Owens clicked the computer mouse, and a screen opened on the monitor. A soldier in uniform could be seen, although the picture was fuzzy.

"Sergeant Stotts," Mr. Owens said loudly, "we don't have a camera, so you can't see us, but you should be able to hear us, and we can see and hear you."

"You're coming through loud and clear, Mr. Owens," Willy said. His voice sounded tinny on the small computer speakers. "Hey, kids!"

Several students shouted greetings, and then Mr. Owens spoke again. "How are conditions in Iraq today?"

"We had to deal with another bombing," Willy said. "This one happened at an army recruiting center. I think sixteen people were killed. The positive thing is, though, that people are still lining up to volunteer and be involved in their country even with threats like this."

"Willy, how long have you been in Iraq?" Mr. Owens asked.

"Eight months," Willy answered. "I had expected to come home after six months, but my time has been extended. A lot of work still needs to be done here. There are three large groups of people and several smaller groups, and they all want to be in charge of running the country. We're trying to teach them how to work together. Sometimes we succeed, and sometimes we don't. Also, we know that terrorists have come to Iraq from other countries to try to keep us from succeeding here. We have to be careful everywhere we go, because we are always targets for those who disagree with our way of doing things in the United States."

Mr. Owens continued the interview, asking, "What is the country of Iraq like?"

"It's large, with many different parts. Some are pure desert, but others, especially by the rivers, are garden spots. Oil wells dominate the southern plains and also the northern hills. In the desert, it can be very hot, well over 100 degrees. During the nights, though, it gets cold. The wind can blow up dust storms that make it impossible to see more than a few inches. We have to work hard to keep our vehicles and other equipment clean from dust and sand."

"Mr. Owens," Wyatt called out, "ask him why we are fighting in Iraq."

Mr. Owens repeated the question, and Willy replied, "Ever since the war between Iran and Iraq in the 1980s, we've known that Saddam Hussein's government was willing to use chemical weapons and other dangerous weapons against other countries and even against the people of Iraq. For years, we've known that Saddam wanted to build an atomic bomb and was trying to develop new ways of killing people with germ warfare. Inspectors were sent to check his military posts, but it was difficult for them to complete their jobs, and so it seemed like he had something big to hide. Finally, in 2003, the president asked Congress for permission to send the army into Iraq, remove Saddam, and find and destroy his weapons. On March 13, 2003, soldiers from the United States and other countries entered Iraq. Saddam went into hiding, and his government fell. Later that year, our soldiers found where he was hiding and captured him. Right now he is on trial for the crimes he committed against his own people, the citizens of Iraq.

"Some chemical weapons have been found, but a lot fewer than we expected. Some of us still think they are well hidden and might eventually be found, but a lot of people think that Saddam exaggerated what he had to try to frighten other people into doing what he wanted. Meanwhile, our job here is to build respect for America and for the way we do things. We want people here to have the same freedoms we have: freedom to say what they believe, freedom to have meetings with others who agree with them, and freedom to help choose the members of their government. Some people say that the people of the Middle East aren't ready for freedom yet, but I disagree. I think people are people, and I think people everywhere should be free."

Several students were shouting out more questions, but the computer picture faded to static and Willy's voice could no longer be heard. Mr. Owens turned to the class and shrugged.

"We can do things today we could never do before," he said apologetically, "but nothing's perfect yet. I think we lost the signal."

"Mr. Owens," Sean demanded, "do you think we should be fighting in Iraq? Don't you think it would be better if my brother and the other soldiers came home? Both my parents feel like the war has gone on for too long and we have nothing else to accomplish there, except for giving the terrorists the chance to kill even more of our soldiers."

Mr. Owens thought for a few seconds before answering.

"People disagree with each other about that, Sean. One of the things we appreciate in this country is the freedom to disagree out loud and to try to persuade each other of what we believe. Willy was saying, I think, that he believes it is worth his effort to help give other people that kind of freedom.

"I will tell you my opinion, but remember, this is just one man's opinion. I think that our leaders have been worried and perhaps even frightened to see new governments appear in the world that didn't believe in freedom. Khomeini in Iran and Saddam in Iraq and the Taliban in Afghanistan all tried to rule their people by taking away freedom instead of giving freedom. Many more countries in the world will be facing big changes in the years to come. I think our government strongly believes that we need to show the people of the Middle East that a country can succeed with freedom, and that people can elect their leaders and talk openly about their government and their country without losing anything important in those countries. Before another country has a big revolution like Iran had twenty-seven years ago, I think the United States wants to prove to the world that freedom works everywhere, not just here."

"I agree," Dr. Branson said. "I have served in Afghanistan, not because I want my country to be in control over there, but because I want its people to have freedom. I do believe that freedom is worth fighting to defend, not just in the United States, but wherever people live."

The bell rang as she finished talking. Mr. Owens said, "We do need to return to our math schedule tomorrow, but I hope we can find time later this week to keep on talking about these important things as well." The students grabbed their books and went through the hall to their following classes.

That afternoon, Curt and Cheyenne were walking home together, since they lived only a block from each other. "I knew your mother was in the National Guard," Curt remarked, "but I didn't realize what she has been doing in the Guard. I guess you must be pretty proud of her."

"I am proud of her," Cheyenne agreed. "It's exciting to think that a doctor from Arkansas can defend freedom on the other side of the world without having to fire a gun."

The two were approaching the Akbar house, where they saw a small group had gathered—Travis and Wyatt and four other boys from another class at school. They were shouting something at the house, although Curt could not hear what they were saying. While he watched, Travis picked up a stone and threw it at the house. It bounced off the wood frame next to the large living room window.

"Hey!" Curt shouted. "Don't do that! You shouldn't be doing that!"

"We're just standing up for freedom," mocked Travis. "We're telling the terrorists to go back home where they belong."

"Yeah," agreed Wyatt. "Don't you remember what Mr. Owens said? We're free to do whatever we want."

"You're not free to throw stones at people," Curt argued.

"Oh, yeah? Well, who's going to stop us?" Wyatt returned. He picked up another stone. "Are you going to stop me? Would you rather have me throw this at the terrorists...or at you?"

"Quick! Call somebody!" Curt pleaded, but Cheyenne had her cell phone out and was dialing even before he spoke. Stalling for time, Curt said, "Why don't you just throw the rock down the street as far as you can? I bet you can't get it past that mailbox."

"I'm not trying for any distance record," Wyatt laughed. "All I want to do is get some terrorists, or maybe some busybodies who don't know how to mind their own business."

"I am minding my business. Taking care of my neighbors is my business." Already Curt saw that Maria was running from down the block, and her older brothers Juan and Eddie were with her. She was also pressing buttons on her phone. At about the same time, Cho Li came around the corner from his house. Curt had forgotten how nearby the Li family lived. Cheyenne was dialing more numbers, and before Wyatt and Travis and the others realized that they were being surrounded, Lakisha and her brother Duwayne had joined Curt and Cheyenne, and still other friends from school were signaling that they were on their way.

"Do you want to talk some more about who is minding whose business?" Curt asked the six boys quietly. "I think we all know who doesn't belong here. Put down your rocks and go home before you get yourselves in trouble." The rest of the growing group nodded and spoke in agreement.

Frowning, Wyatt dropped the rock he was holding. As he walked past Curt, he tried to bump shoulders with him, but Curt saw what Wyatt was planning and stepped out of the way. As the group watched, the six boys walked down the street away from the Akbar house.

Cheyenne looked at the house and saw a girl standing behind the living room window. The girl had a long scarf wrapped around her head, but Cheyenne could see the girl's bright, sparkling eyes. Shyly, Shiraz waved to Cheyenne and then pulled the drapes closed. Cheyenne waved back, hoping that Shiraz was watching through the crack between the drapes. Suddenly, Cheyenne was looking forward to the rest of the week at school, with the exciting hope of making a new friend.

After Iraq invaded Kuwait in August 1990, thirty-four nations sent soldiers to defend Kuwait. From the United States, 2,225,000 soldiers were sent to the conflict; 147 American soldiers died. From Arkansas, at least 3,400 soldiers served in the first Gulf War, and at least four are known to have died.

The terrorist attack in New York and Washington DC on September 11, 2001, killed 2,974 people from ninety different countries (but most of them Americans) in the buildings that were attacked and in the airplanes that were used as weapons (including the one that crashed in rural Pennsylvania). Since that time, 58,250 American soldiers and 43,750 from other nations have served in various capacities in Afghanistan during and after the battles of 2001, alongside the army of Afghanistan, which includes roughly 90,000 soldiers. They have been opposed by Taliban and other forces estimated at the end of 2008 to be no more than 10,000 surviving fighters. Five thousand Afghan soldiers and 1,305 soldiers from the United States and other nations have died in Afghanistan since October 2001; roughly 23,000 opponents are thought to have been killed in various battles during that time.

During the second Gulf War, 368,620 soldiers from the United States and other nations faced an Iraqi army of about 375,000 soldiers. One hundred seventy-one soldiers from the United States and Great Britain died in the invasion, during which an unknown number (estimated from 10,000 to 30,000) Iraqi soldiers and civilians also died. Since the invasion, the number of American and other soldiers has varied but generally has been roughly half the size of the invasion force, and 4,549 soldiers from the United States and other nations have died in Iraq during that time.

Since 2001, 15,387 soldiers from Arkansas have served in one fashion or another in southwest Asia. As of 2009, seventy-seven soldiers from Arkansas have died while serving there.

ABOUT THE AUTHORS

Velma B. Branscum Woody grew up with a love of history given to her by her grandfather, Charlie Branscum. Mrs. Woody has taught high school history, including Arkansas history, for twenty years and has taught history at several universities throughout the state. She has a BSE degree, an MSE degree, and twenty-one hours toward a doctorate. Her book *Bandits, Bears, and Backaches* was published by the Butler Center in 2004. Currently, Mrs. Woody is an adjunct professor at Ozarka College. She lives in north Arkansas on a farm near Onia, surrounded by her five children and five grandchildren.

Steven Teske works on the staff of the Encyclopedia of Arkansas History & Culture at the Butler Center for Arkansas Studies, located in the Arkansas Studies Institute in Little Rock. He is also an adjunct instructor for the Arkansas State University–Beebe campus located at the Little Rock Air Force Base in Jacksonville, and has taught classes for Pulaski Technical College at their Little Rock campus. Mr. Teske lives with his wife and seven children in North Little Rock.

Lightning Source UK Ltd.
Milton Keynes UK
05 December 2009

147108UK00001B/4/P